# The
# LIBERTY
## Book of
# SIMPLE
# SEWING

**TEXT BY LUCINDA GANDERTON & CHRISTINE LEECH**

Photography by Kristin Perers, Illustrations by Lucinda Ganderton

ALHAMBRA
EDITIONS

**PROJECTS CONCEIVED AND MADE BY**
Lucinda Ganderton and Christine Leech

**PUBLISHING DIRECTOR** Jane O'Shea
**COMMISSIONING EDITOR** Lisa Pendreigh
**EDITOR** Alison Wormleighton
**CREATIVE DIRECTOR** Helen Lewis
**ART DIRECTION & DESIGN** Claire Peters
**DESIGNER** Jim Smith
**ILLUSTRATOR** Lucinda Ganderton
**PHOTOGRAPHER** Kristin Perers
**STYLIST** Twig Hutchinson
**MODELS** Alex Marshall at FM London, Benjamin,
Aurelie and Basil
**PRODUCTION DIRECTOR** Vincent Smith
**PRODUCTION CONTROLLER** Sarah Neesam

Quadrille
*craft*

www.quadrillecraft.com

This edition first published in 2013 by
Alhambra Editions
Alhambra House
27–31 Charing Cross Road
London WC2H 0LS
www.quadrille.co.uk

British Library Cataloguing-in-Publication Data
A catalogue record for this book is available from
the British Library.

ISBN: 978 184949 475 5

Reprinted in 2014
10 9 8 7 6 5 4 3 2

Printed in China.

# CONTENTS

# INTRODUCTION

Sewing really doesn't need to be complicated. In fact, if you can sew a line of straight stitches then you can make a surprisingly large number of sewn items for your home – curtains, throws and cushions, for starters. Add curved seams and slip stitching hems into your sewing repertoire and you will have the skills to make the majority of projects in this book, from the largest curtain panel on pages 24–27 to the smallest rag doll on pages 80–87. You don't need to be a skilled seamstress to achieve professional looking results as the projects have all been designed with the novice stitcher in mind, and yet the more experienced maker will undoubtedly find items to spark their sewing imaginations.

Liberty has always been a byword for quality, style and even luxury. Progressive yet traditional, Liberty Art Fabrics are unique in marrying the contemporary with the timeless. This is reflected in THE LIBERTY BOOK OF SIMPLE SEWING, which offers the home sewer a chance to add an element of Liberty style to their interior through the over 25 simple sewing projects. The traditional techniques of hand quilting, for example, are married with the contemporary graphic lines of the chevron on pages 70–75, but also provide the perfect showcase for a range of tonal Liberty Lifestyle craft fabrics.

THE LIBERTY BOOK OF SIMPLE SEWING has been created to showcase the variety of Liberty Art Fabrics designed prints, to inspire the reader with their versatility and to provide an irresistible collection of original designs to create for the home. The range of projects includes core items, such as cushions, as well as more unexpected designs like the graffiti table runner, but they are all characterised by the imaginative use of fabric with often unique combinations of the colour and pattern.

Projects such as the no-sew patchwork picture frames on pages 34–37 or the floral garland on pages 88–91 can easily be accomplished in an afternoon, and can even be made from scraps of fabric left over from other projects. At the other end of the spectrum, makes such as the striped throw on pages 144–149 are more labour-intensive investment pieces that are set to become cherished family keepsakes.

# ESSENTIAL TOOLS & EQUIPMENT

Haberdashery departments, quilt shops and online craft stores are full of tempting gadgets, but when assembling your sewing kit bear in mind that you only need a few basic items to make any project in this book. Quality tools, however, are an investment; they will help you achieve a professional result and last for many years. Keep everything organised in a lidded box or make the multi-pocketed sewing tidy on pages 108–113 to keep your equipment to hand.

## NEEDLES

There is a special type of needle for each hand sewing task, so start off with a large assorted packet. They come in various thicknesses: the larger the number the more slender the needle, and you'll soon find a personal preference. Store them safely in a needlebook or keep them in the packet – they tend to disappear into pincushions.

- 'Sharps' are used for most hand stitching and tacking. They are medium length and have a small round eye to accommodate a single strand of sewing thread.

- 'Betweens' or 'quilting' needles are shorter and finer, and will easily slide through several layers of fabric.

- 'Crewel' needles have long eyes for stranded embroidery cotton. This makes them easy to thread and suitable for all general sewing.

## THIMBLES

Thimbles and other finger-guards give vital protection if you are doing a lot of hand stitching and are essential for quilting when you may need one on each hand. If you haven't used one before, it may feel clumsy and ungainly, but do persevere. Steel thimbles come in different sizes, so you should be able to find one that is comfortable but lightweight silicone thimbles are best of all, moulding to fit your fingertip snugly.

## PINS

Steel dressmaker's pins are 2.5–3.5cm long with tiny heads. They are very fine, so leave no marks in the fabric – ideal for Liberty Tana Lawn. Glass-headed pins, however, are easier to handle and show up well against patterned fabrics. Store your pins in a tin (along with a small magnet) or a pincushion.

## SAFETY PINS

Large safety pins are used for threading ribbon or elastic through casings – you'll need one for the drawstring bag on pages 137–139 or the waistband of the children's pyjama trousers on pages 118–123. Quilter's safety pins are an invaluable alternative to traditional tacking when putting a quilt together. Their curved shape makes them easy to insert through the three layers of fabric and wadding.

## CUTTING AND SNIPPING

You'll need three different sized pairs of scissors: each does a very different job.

- Tailor's shears are used for fabric, but never paper which will blunt the long steel blades. The angled handles keep the lower blade flat against the table for precise cutting of large shapes. Look out for a pair with comfortable cushioned handles.

- Medium household scissors can be used for cutting out smaller fabric items and for all of your paper patterns and templates.

- Small embroidery scissors with a sharp point are ideal for snipping threads, notching seams and clipping corners.

A round-bladed rotary cutter is always used with a clear plastic quilter's ruler and a self-healing plastic mat. These tools are often used for patchwork, but are a very quick and accurate means of preparing larger squares and rectangles to given measurements.

## MEASURING TOOLS

A long flexible tape measure is vital, and spring-loaded retractable ones are the tidiest. Also, a short plastic ruler is handy for checking hem lengths and seam widths.

## MARKING TOOLS

Air-erasable pens are a great innovation: their light sensitive pigment fades in time, and so they can be used to draw seam allowances, pattern markings or embroidery outlines on the finest fabrics without leaving any trace of ink. Traditional tailor's chalk shows up on darker and thicker fabrics, and a sharp HB pencil provides a light outline on areas that will be covered.

### IRONING

Iron your fabric well to remove any creases before cutting out and press each seam as you work, so keep your iron and board in your workspace. A mist spray helps steam out stubborn creases whilst fabric stiffener or spray starch gives extra body to fine fabrics.

### FIXING AND GLUING

In addition to your sewing kit, you'll need some basic craft equipment. The fabric on the patchwork picture frames on pages 34–37 is glued with PVA, a water-soluble liquid adhesive that dries to a clear finish. Double-sided tape is used to secure the fabric cover on the drum lampshade on pages 66–69. The upholstered footstool on pages 140–143 requires a small hammer and decorative nails, and the covered letters on pages 38–43 need a staple gun.

### THREAD

Keep a reel of white poly-cotton thread in your sewing box, and a few bright colours for easily identifiable tacking. When buying thread for a particular project, you should match the colour to the fabric as closely as possible. If you can't find an exact match go for a slightly darker shade. Match fibre to fibre when choosing your thread: finely spun mercerised cotton thread is best for sewing Liberty Tana Lawn, and poly-cotton works well with heavier Linen Union and Kingly Cord. Use quilting thread for sewing together the layers of throws and quilts.

### FUSIBLE BONDING WEB

This heat-sensitive adhesive comes on a paper backing. Use it for tracing, cutting and bonding intricate appliqué shapes and also to fix two layers of fabric together for projects like the floral garland on pages 88–91 or the pockets on the picnic bag on pages 124–129.

### FILLINGS AND STUFFINGS

Furnishing suppliers offer a wide selection of ready-made cushion pads with feather, cotton or synthetic fillings in standard shapes. Stuff one-off shapes, like the cloud cushions on pages 18–21, with polyester cushion fibre, but always check that it meets safety standards before buying. The same applies to toy stuffing – in case of mishaps, this should be washable. Flat cushions, like the chair pads on pages 28–33, have a 2cm upholstery foam filling which can be cut with scissors. Specialist suppliers can cut deeper foam to size.

## GETTING STARTED

### DRAFTING THE PATTERNS

Many of the projects – including the table mats and leaf cushions – are constructed from simple strips, squares and rectangles. The dimensions for these are given in the 'cutting out' section. To make a pattern for these shapes, mark the width and depth onto dressmaker's squared paper (like an oversized sheet of graph paper with a 1cm grid) and cut out along the printed lines. Alternatively – and more speedily – use a rotary cutter, a quilter's ruler and a cutting mat.

Small shaped templates – like those for the Libby doll and her outfit on pages 80–87 – are given as half-size outlines that you can photocopy directly from the page, enlarging them at 200%. Larger patterns, such as the children's pyjama trousers, are shown in a scaled-down version on a square grid. Draw these to full size on dressmaker's squared paper, copying the line within each small square onto its larger equivalent. Copy the markings onto your paper pattern and label each piece clearly.

The size and shape of other projects are variable and will depend on the size of your window or lampshade. Clear guidance is given for measuring up and working out the proportions for these items.

Before you cut out the fabric for any of the projects, always double check that your pattern is the correct size.

### WORKING WITH FABRIC

Look closely at any piece of fabric and you'll see that it's made up of two sets of interwoven threads, which lie at right angles to each other. The long threads that are set onto the loom are known as the warp and they run from top to bottom of the finished cloth, as the 'long grain'. The threads that are woven between them are called the weft, and run from left to right, as the 'side grain'. The woven edges are known as the selvedges. Always cut these away, as the fabric here is more tightly woven.

Your pattern pieces should always be positioned so that the side edges are parallel to the selvedges, and they lie squarely along the 'long grain' of the fabric. Pieces that are not cut on the grain can stretch and become distorted.

Many of the Liberty Tana Lawns and Liberty Lifestyle craft fabrics have small-scale overall patterns, so the actual position of the templates isn't critical, but on larger designs they should be placed so that the design lines up on each piece. You'll need to allow extra fabric for this, and also if you are making a set of matching chair pads. Centre large motifs and if you are working with stripes or ginghams, make sure you keep the patterns parallel with the lines.

### CUTTING OUT
Press your material to get rid of any creases before you pin on the patterns, then smooth it out flat on your work surface. The double-ended arrow on the pattern indicates the direction of the grain and this should always point from top to bottom of the fabric. Cut out around the outside edges of the pattern with your shears, keeping the angled handle downwards and making smooth strokes.

### KNOW YOUR SEWING MACHINE
You may be an experienced stitcher with a trusted workhorse of a machine, but for the new enthusiast the variety of machines in a department store can be confusing. These range from simple plastic entry-level versions to high-tech computerised models. Go to a reputable dealer, try them all out and spend time talking to the knowledgeable sales team – but don't be tempted to overspend. Study the manual carefully – it tells you all the technical information and will have a useful trouble shooting section.

All that's needed for simple sewing projects is a reliable machine with a few basic functions: the ability to cope with thicker fabrics, a zigzag stitch for neatening seams and a regular straight stitch with an even tension. Use the basic foot for everything except sewing in zips – you won't need the buttonhole foot or the more specialised dressmaking feet for the straightforward sewing in this book.

Some machines will automatically adjust the presser foot when sewing different weight fabrics, but on others you have to change a lever. Don't forget to do this, as a fine fabric like Liberty Tana Lawn needs less pressure than Liberty Linen Union. Always match the gauge of the needle to the material being sewn: fine for lawn cotton and a thicker one for canvas or heavy calico. Change the needles regularly, as a blunt or snagged point causes irregular stitches. And if your machine doesn't come with a hard case, you can always stitch your own cover using the instructions on pages 134–137.

## HEMS AND BINDING

There are two ways to finish off an edge: by turning it back and stitching down the fold to make a hem or by binding it with a narrow strip of fabric.

### SINGLE HEM
Neaten the edge of the fabric with a zigzag or overlock stitch. With the right side facing downwards, fold the edge back to the given depth, pressing it with a hot iron as you go. Use a ruler to keep this measurement constant. Pin the turning down, then machine stitch just below the zigzag, or stitch by hand.

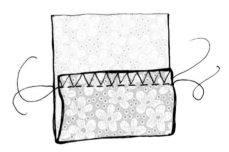

### DOUBLE HEM
This more durable finish is made up of two turnings and is used for curtains and garments. Fold and press the first turning as above, then measure and press a second turning to conceal the raw edge. Pin and tack, then hem stitch or sew down 3mm from the inner fold.

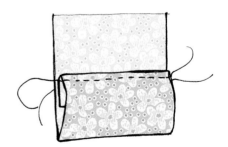

### BOUND EDGE

To bind the edges of a quilt you can use ready-made bias binding (which you can buy in a range of Liberty prints) or make your own straight binding from matching or contrasting fabric. Cut a long, narrow strip four times the finished depth. Press it in half, then press the raw edges to the centre crease and unfold.

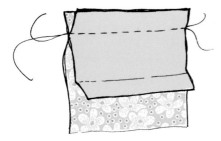

Pin the binding along the edge of the quilt with the right sides facing and raw edges matching. Machine stitch along the first crease line.

Re-fold the bottom crease, turn the binding over to the back and tack down. Slip stitch the fold or machine stitch just inside the edge of the binding. To bind a curved edge, like those on the cafetière cover on pages 62–65 you will need to use ready-made bias binding and stretch it gently to fit around the corners.

## SEAMS AND JOINS

Before two pieces of fabric are seamed together they have to be joined temporarily with pins and/or tacking. Hold them both together with right sides facing and match up the edges. Insert a pin at each corner, then along the rest of the edge. You can position the pins parallel to the edge or if you are not going to tack the seam, put them in at right angles, so that they can easily be pulled out as the fabric passes under the presser foot. A line of tacking – large running stitches – makes a stable foundation for machine stitching. Sew just inside the seam line with a contrasting thread that will be unpicked when the seam is complete.

The width of the seam allowance – the spare fabric that lies within a seam – is specified for each individual project. For Liberty Tana Lawn or Liberty Lifestyle craft fabric it's usually 10mm, or 15mm for heavier fabrics. Like all patchwork, the chevron quilt blocks are joined with a narrow 6mm seam. To keep this width consistent, line the raw edges up against the corresponding parallel line, which you'll find etched onto the sewing machine's base plate. Hold the fabric in this position as you guide it under the presser foot.

Press each seam as it is completed to give your work a crisp finish. Sometimes the seam allowance is pressed to one side, but where a flat finish is required the seam is pressed open. Do this by gently parting the two sides of the allowance with the toe of the iron.

### STRAIGHT SEAM

With right sides facing, sew the two edges together with the given seam allowance. It's always a good idea to reinforce both ends of the seam line with a few reverse stitches so that the ends don't come undone. Press the seam allowance open or to one side as directed.

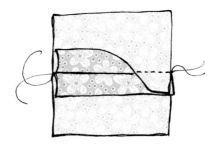

## FRENCH SEAM

This enclosed seam gives a neat look on both back and front, and is used to make the curtain panel on pages 24–27. Pin the two edges together with wrong sides facing and join with a 1cm seam. Now trim the allowance back to 4mm and refold the fabric so that the right sides are facing and the raw edges lie inside. For accuracy you can tack the front and back together, making sure the seam lies along the edge. Stitch the seam again, taking the required allowance, then press the seam to one side.

## OVERLOCKED SEAM

Garment seams are neatened on the inside to prevent them fraying when washed. After stitching a straight seam, trim the allowance as necessary then zigzag or overlock the two edges together before pressing.

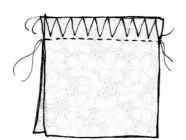

## TOP STITCHED SEAM

Top stitching reinforces a seam and gives a neat finish. After stitching a straight seam, press the seam allowance to one side then sew through all three layers on the right side, 3mm from the seam line, using the inside space on the presser foot as a guide.

## OUTSIDE CURVED SEAM

This technique is used for the edged pillowcase on pages 102–107 and the cloud cushions and mobile on pages 18–23. Start by trimming the seam allowance down to 6mm.

Around an outside curve, cut out a series of tiny triangles to within 3mm of the stitch line to reduce the bulk. This enables the seam to lie flat when it is turned right side out and pressed.

## CORNER SEAM

Stitch along the seam allowance as far as the corner. Keeping the needle down, raise the presser foot. Pivot the fabric, then continue along the next edge. Reduce the bulk by trimming away a triangle of surplus fabric at the corner. Turn right side out and gently ease out the point with a knitting needle or a pencil.

## REINFORCING STITCHES

Straps and handles, such as the dog lead on pages 48–49 for instance, need to be stitched down in a way that gives them extra strength. Press under a 1cm turning and tack in place. Starting at the bottom left corner, machine stitch a rectangle across the end, then stitch up to the top right corner, across to the top left corner, down to bottom right and back to the start point. You may find it helpful to mark the outline first.

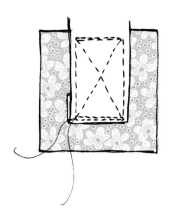

## INSIDE CURVED SEAM

Make a row of little snips into the seam allowance along an inside curve. Cut right into the space between two adjacent curves. Use this technique for the edged pillowcase on pages 102–107 and the cloud cushions and mobile on pages 18–23.

# HAND STITCHING

### HAND STITCHES

Careful preparation and hand finishing give a professional finish to any needlework project, so here are the four basic stitches that you will need to seam, gather, tack, add trimmings and close up gaps.

### RUNNING STITCH

This simple stitch is used for joining, gathering and quilting. The spaces and stitches are equal and the length is between 5mm and 8mm depending on the thickness of the cloth. With practice, and using a long needle, you should be able to pick up two or three stitches at a time. Make longer stitches when tacking, or use the dressmaker's variation below. A line of running stitch is used for gathering by hand and the thread is pulled up to create a frill.

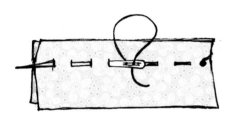

### DRESSMAKER'S TACKING

A temporary line of tacking holds two pieces of fabric together before they are sewn by machine. The length of the individual stitches doesn't really matter as long as the seam is aligned accurately, but generally they should be about 2cm for thick fabrics and 1cm for finer materials. The stitches are about twice as long as the spaces between them.

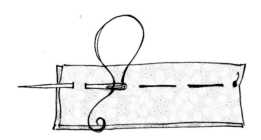

### OVER STITCH

Use this stitch for sewing on braids, such as the bobble fringing that embellishes the chair pads. Work a line of short diagonal stitches over the edge of the trimming, in a matching thread.

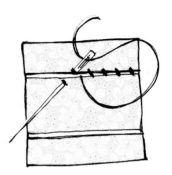

### SLIP STITCH

This joining stitch produces a flat, unobtrusive seam. It's used to hold together two folded edges on either side of an opening, like that on the cloud cushions.

Bring the needle out through the bottom fold and, keeping it roughly horizontal, insert the point through the top fold, directly above the start point. Push the tip through the top fold so that it emerges 5–7mm further along, then pull the needle through. Insert it directly below and repeat the same action to the end of the seam.

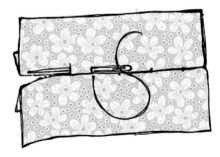

Slip stitch can also be used to attach a folded edge to a flat, single layer. Bring the needle out through the folded edge and insert it into the single, flat layer directly above. Make a stitch picking up only about three threads, then push the needle through the folded edge so it emerges 5–7mm further along. Repeat.

## PATCHWORK & APPLIQUÉ

A patchwork quilt consists of three layers: the pieced top which is made up from individual patches, the wadding or batting that gives it warmth and thickness, and the plain backing fabric.

The patches for the chevron quilt are quickly and easily cut on a self-healing mat, with a standard 6 inch quilter's square and a sharp rotary cutter. Replace the blades regularly, as they dull with use or can become nicked. Patchwork is traditionally stitched with a 6mm seam. This distance is marked on most presser feet, or you can buy a specially designed narrow foot to keep a regular seam.

There are several types of wadding for the centre layer of the quilt sandwich. Thick polyester is tactile and puffy, and easy to wash and dry for everyday use. Natural cotton and bamboo fibres are lighter and give a soft, draped look to the finished quilt. They will shrink slightly when laundered and the slightly puckered effect that this produces gives depth and texture to the quilt.

You can join two lengths of fabric for the back of your quilt, but 'whole cloth', or a single width, saves time. Look out for an old bed sheet in good condition or buy new sheeting or extra-wide fabric in a colour to complement the quilt top.

## QUILTING

Once you have assembled the three layers (the project step-by-step instructions tell you just how to do this) it's time to handquilt. Use tightly spun quilting thread for this and a short, slender needle. Quilting stitch is simply a small, regular running stitch, which is worked either 'in the ditch' – along the seam line between patches – or 4–6mm outside the seam, as an outline. You'll find your own preferred way of working after a while, with one hand above and one below the quilt. Roll up the area not being used and place it either on the table in front of you, or over your lap to keep you cosy in the colder months.

Start each length of thread invisibly in the traditional way. Make a tiny knot at one end and insert the needle at the start point. Gently pull the thread and you'll feel the knot 'pop' through the fabric. Work a back stitch to secure it, then sew along the quilting line. Finish off with three tiny back stitches, one over the other, and take the needle through the wadding. Bring it up 3cm away and clip the end close to the surface. With a bit of wiggling about it will disappear neatly into the quilt.

Small projects like the cafetière cover can be machine quilted with closely spaced parallel lines. Make sure that the layers are tacked or pinned together well before machine stitching or they will slide around. Larger quilted items need a special 'walking foot' which minimises the risk of movement.

## APPLIQUÉ

### FUSIBLE BONDING WEB
This invaluable aid to appliqué is a heat-sensitive adhesive mounted on paper. It melts under the heat of an iron to fuse two layers of fabric together and comes in heavy- and light-bond weights. Choose a heavy bond for thicker fabrics and light bond for Tana Lawn, such as on the leaf cushions on pages 96–101.

Bearing in mind that the motif has to be reversed, trace the outline onto the paper side of the bonding web and cut the shape out roughly. Following the manufacturer's instructions, press the adhesive onto the appliqué fabric, then cut out around the pencil line. Peel off the backing paper, position the motif, – the right way up – on the backing fabric and press down. Use an up-and-down action rather than a sliding motion to prevent any distortion of the appliqué motif. Finish off the raw edges with a narrow machine satin stitch in a matching or contrasting colour thread. Some machines have a blanket or feather stitch function, which will give a more decorative look.

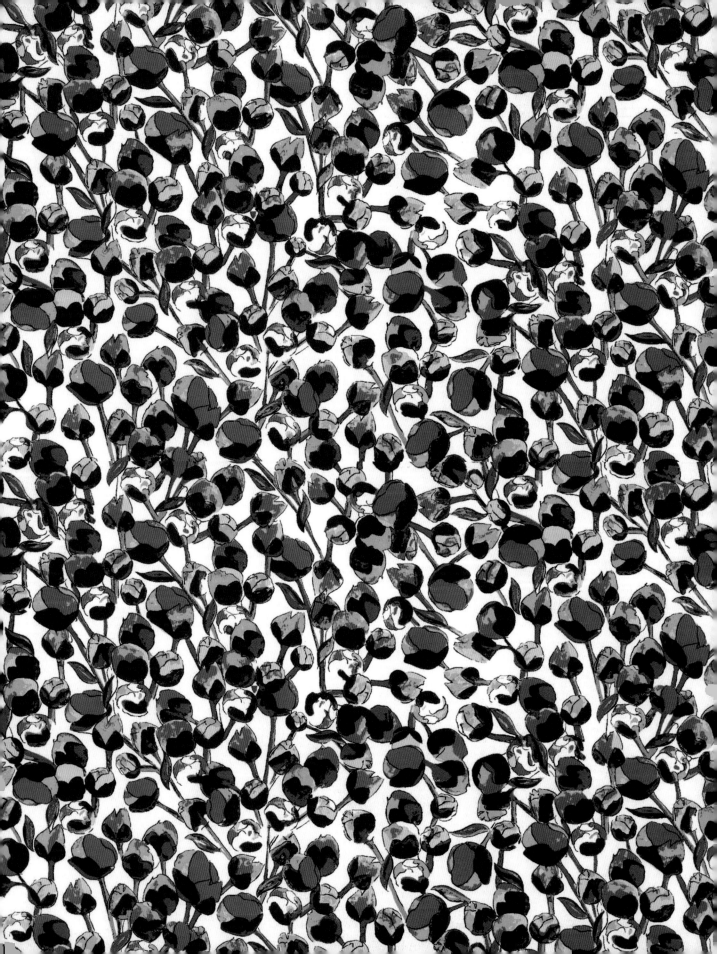

PROJECTS

# CLOUD CUSHIONS

*All you need is one metre or less of medium-weight cotton fabric in your favourite print to make a cute cumulus-shaped cushion.*

**YOU WILL NEED**

### for the large cushion
- 70 x 90cm Liberty Lifestyle craft fabric in print of your choice (we used Garnett in colourway C)

### for the medium cushion
- 110 x 35cm Liberty Lifestyle craft fabric in print of your choice (we used Woolf in colourway C)

### for the small cushion
- 100 x 30cm Liberty Lifestyle craft fabric in print of your choice (we used in Catherine colourway C)

**FOR ALL SIZE CUSHIONS YOU WILL NEED**
- matching sewing thread
- 500g safety standard polyester cushion filling
- sewing machine
- sewing kit

**TEMPLATE**

Copy the template on page 151, enlarging it by 250%, 325% or 400%, depending on the size cushion.

**CUTTING OUT**

*from Liberty Lifestyle craft fabric*
two clouds in your chosen size (one reversed)

*The large, medium and small cushions are made in the same way, regardless of size.*

**GARNETT** *is based on several 1930s Liberty designs. It was first printed at Liberty's Merton Abbey Print Works on wool in 1971.*

## ❶ PINNING THE COVER TOGETHER

Place the two clouds together with the right sides facing inwards. Match up the curves and pin round the outside edge, leaving a 15cm gap at the bottom.

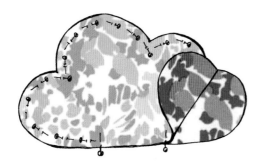

## ❷ SEWING AND TRIMMING THE SEAM

Sew the cushion together with a 15mm seam. To maintain a consistent width, you should line the edge of the fabric up with the 15mm mark on the footplate as you sew. Start at the left edge of the gap and reinforce both ends of the seam with a few reverse stitches. Trim the seam allowance back to 1cm all round.

## ❸ NOTCHING THE SEAM ALLOWANCE

Now cut out a series of small notches around each curve to create a smooth outline. Cut to within 2mm of the stitch line and space the notches about 4cm apart; closer together on the tighter curves. Snip a deep 'v' shape at the inward points where the curves meet.

## ❹ TURNING THE COVER RIGHT SIDE OUT

Press back the 1cm seam allowance along the bottom edge, then turn the cover right side out through the opening. Ease out the curved seams, then press the cover, pulling gently on the inward points to allow the fabric to stretch.

## ❺ FILLING THE CUSHION WITH STUFFING

Fill the cover with the polyester cushion filling. Keep a continuous stream of stuffing going into the cushion and push it right up into each curve; do not break the stuffing off in clumps as the cushion can become oddly lumpy.

## ❻ SEWING UP THE OPENING

Pin the two sides of the opening together. Using small neat slip stitches, hand sew it closed. Mould the finished cushion with your hands to distribute the filling evenly within the cover. Pass a warm iron over the curves to remove any remaining creases.

# CLOUD MOBILE

*After sewing the cloud cushions, you'll find yourself left with some corner scraps of spare fabric, which are perfect for making this mobile.*

**YOU WILL NEED**

- 60 x 20cm turquoise cotton fabric
- 50 x 15cm Liberty Lifestyle craft fabric in three prints of your choice (we used the corner remnants of Catherine in colourway C, Garnet in colourway C and Woolf in colourway C left over from making the Cloud Cushions)
- 28 assorted clear and blue glass drop beads
- 28 round 3mm silver glass beads
- safety standard polyester cushion or toy filling
- matching sewing thread
- silver sewing thread
- silver ring, for hanging
- sewing machine
- sewing kit

**TEMPLATE**
Copy the template on page 151, enlarging it by 130% for the small cloud and 160% for the large cloud.

**CUTTING OUT**

*from turquoise cotton fabric*
two large clouds (one reversed)

*from each Liberty Lifestyle craft fabric*
two small clouds (one reversed)

**❶ MAKING THE CLOUDS**
These tiny clouds are made in the same way as the Cloud Cushions, so refer to the detailed instructions on page 20. Pin and tack the two pieces together with right sides facing and stitch with a 1cm seam, leaving a 6cm opening along the bottom edge.

**❷** Trim the seam allowance back to 6mm and notch the curves. Press back the bottom seam allowance, turn right side out and ease out the seams. Press lightly, stuff with polyester filling and slip stitch the opening.

### ❸ ADDING THE RAINDROPS

Sew seven glass drops at 2–3cm intervals along the bottom edge of each small cloud. Thread a fine needle with silver sewing thread and secure the end to the seam line. Add a small round bead, then a glass drop. Take the needle back up through the round bead and re-insert at the start point. Pull up the thread until the strand is 5–8cm long.

**❹** Secure the strand with two small stitches, then pass the needle back through the cloud and out again 2–3cm further along the seam line, ready for the next bead. Hang the largest bead at the centre.

### ❺ GETTING THE RIGHT BALANCE

Fasten a 40cm length of silver sewing thread to the top of each cloud, in line with the large dots marked on the templates. Make a hanging loop for the large cloud by passing the thread through the metal ring and sewing it back onto the cloud.

**❻** Attach the small clouds to the three dots at the bottom edge, but don't fasten off the hanging threads just yet. Draw up the centre cloud so the thread is about 8cm long and the other two measure approximately 20cm and 25cm. Wrap the ends of the thread around pins to keep them at the right length, then hang up the mobile. Adjust the length of the threads (and possibly their positions) until all four clouds hang straight: this step involves a bit of trial and error. Secure the threads in their final positions.

### ❼ FINISHING OFF

Add the remaining beads to the bottom edge of the large cloud, spacing them evening between the hanging threads.

# CURTAIN PANEL

*Use the full widths of both the linen
fabric and your chosen Liberty print
to make this delightfully floaty curtain,
which filters light and provides privacy.*

**YOU WILL NEED**

- 80 x 135cm plain fine linen fabric
- 135 x 50cm Liberty Tana Lawn in print of your choice (we used Marina Seaflower in colourway D)
- matching sewing thread
- sewing machine
- sewing kit
- expanding café curtain pole to fit inside your window frame

**MEASURING UP**

Finished width = 135cm
Finished drop = half the height of the window

Our curtain is 100cm long: reduce the depth of the main panel to make a shorter curtain and reduce the width of each piece to make a narrower curtain.

**CUTTING OUT**

Label each piece as you cut it out, so they don't get mixed up.

### from plain fine linen fabric

| | |
|---|---|
| main panel | one 135 x 65cm rectangle |
| strip 2 | one 135 x 8cm strip |
| strip 4 | one 135 x 7cm strip |

### from Liberty Tana Lawn

| | |
|---|---|
| strip 1 | one 135 x 13cm strip |
| strip 3 | one 135 x 10cm strip |
| strip 5 | one 135 x 8cm strip |
| binding | two 4cm x length of finished depth + 2cm strips |
| casing | one 138 x 7cm strip |
| | one 4 x 7cm rectangle |

## ❶ HEMMING THE FIRST TANA LAWN STRIP

Press under a 1cm turning along the bottom edge of Strip 1. Fold and press the neatened edge once again to make a double hem. Pin the turning and machine stitch it down, 3mm from the fold.

## ❷ JOINING ON A LINEN STRIP

The strips are all joined with French seams, which enclose the raw edges and give a neat finish on both sides of the curtain. Pin Strip 2 to the wrong side of Strip 1 and machine stitch the two together 8mm from the edge. Trim the seam allowance down to 4mm.

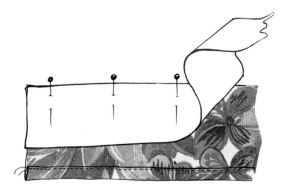

### ❸ COMPLETING THE FRENCH SEAM

Turn both pieces of fabric back, so that the right sides are together and press the seam so that the stitch line lies at the outside edge. Tack them both and machine stitch 8mm from this edge.

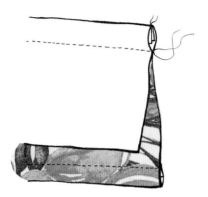

### ❹ ADDING THE OTHER STRIPS

Join on Strips 3, 4 and 5 in the same way, then sew the top edge of Strip 5 to the bottom edge of the main panel. Press each seam so that the allowances lie over the Tana Lawn.

### ❺ BINDING THE EDGES

Press under a 6mm turning along one long edge of each binding strip. With right sides together, pin the raw edge of one strip to one side edge of the curtain, leaving a 1cm overlap at the bottom corner. Machine stitch in place, taking a 6mm seam allowance.

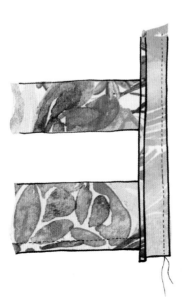

### ❻

Press back the overlap in line with the hem. Turn the binding to the wrong side of the curtain and pin so that the edge lies just inside the stitch line. Slip stitch down the fold, taking care not to let the stitches show on the right side.

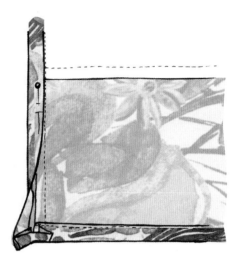

### ❼ MAKING THE CASING

With right sides facing, pin and stitch the extra piece to the casing strip, taking a 6mm seam allowance. Press the seam open. Press and machine stitch a narrow double hem at each short edge, adjusting the length to match the curtain. Press under an 8mm turning along one long edge. With right sides facing, pin and stitch the raw edge to the top edge of the curtain. Finish off as for the side bindings. Slot the pole through the casing and adjust to fit inside the window.

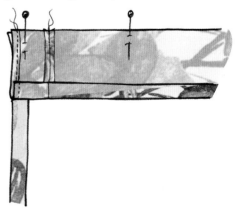

# CHAIR PADS

—•—

*Enliven plain metal or wooden kitchen
chairs with made-to-measure seat pads,
which provide colour as well as comfort.*

**YOU WILL NEED**

*for each chair pad*
- approximately 50cm square Liberty Linen Union in print of your choice (we used Hebe in colourway A)
- approximately 50cm square plain furnishing fabric in contrasting or matching colour, for the backing
- approximately 40cm of 2.5cm-deep safety standard foam
- 1m bobble edging in contrasting colour
- 40cm self-adhesive magnetic strip or 1m cotton tape, for the optional ties

- permanent marker pen
- air-erasable pen or chalk pencil
- large sheet of card (if fabric has a large pattern)
- matching sewing thread
- sheet of newspaper
- sewing machine
- sewing kit

Note: If you are using a fabric with a large repeat pattern, like the one shown here, you will need to allow extra length if all your pads are to be identical.

**HEBE** *is a one-colour version of Liberty's famous peacock feather pattern.
This design has been in the range since the 1890s and is one of the key
prints associated with Liberty.*

# ❶ MAKING THE TEMPLATES

Cut a sheet of newspaper roughly to the size of your chair seat, tape it to your chair and draw around the outside edge of the seat. Cut along this line. To make the template symmetrical, fold the newspaper in half vertically and trim both edges. This process may take a bit of trial and error, but you will end up with a perfect fit. If you want your cushion to have ties, mark the position of the two outer struts on the template.

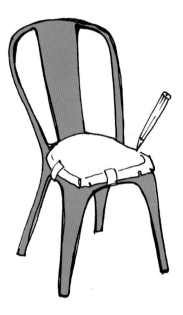

❷ Place the paper template centrally on the sheet of card, draw around the edge and neatly cut out to create a window template. You can now line up this frame on your fabric to select the area of pattern. If your print does not have a large repeat, omit this step and simply use the newspaper template.

# ❸ CUTTING OUT THE CHAIR PAD FRONT

Position the window template on the wrong side of the print fabric and move it around to find an interesting, symmetrical section of the pattern. Draw around the inside of the template, using a chalk pencil for a dark fabric or an air-erasable marker for a light fabric.

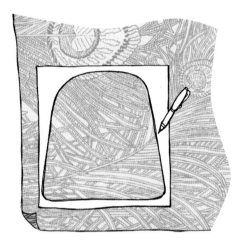

# ❹ ADDING THE ALLOWANCES

To allow for the depth of the foam, you will need to add on an extra 1cm all round plus a 1cm seam allowance. Using a clear ruler or quilter's square as a guide, draw a line 2cm outside your marked outline. Cut neatly around this line.

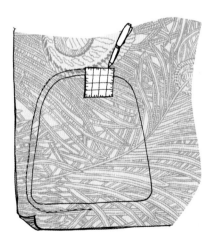

## ❺ MAKING UP THE COVER

Pin the chair pad front to the backing fabric, with right sides facing, leaving a 15cm opening at the top edge. If you are adding ties, cut the tape in half and then fold each length in half. Referring back to the template, pin the folds to the edge of the chair pad front, in line with the strut marks. Tack the front and backing together, then machine stitch 1cm from the edge, leaving the 15cm opening unstitched. Reinforce both ends of the seam with a few reverse stitches. Trim the backing fabric in line with the chair pad front.

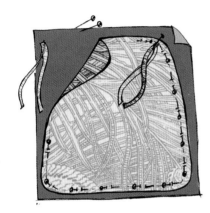

## ❻ NOTCHING THE CORNERS

For perfectly smooth curves at the corners, you will need to notch the seam allowance. Cut a series of small triangles from the surplus fabric to within 3mm of the stitch line, spacing them approximately 2cm apart.

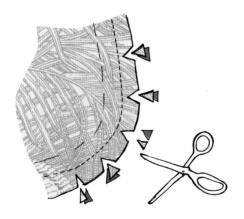

## ❼ TURNING THE COVER RIGHT SIDE OUT

Press back the seam allowance along either side of the top opening, then turn the cover right side out through the opening. Ease out the seams and lightly press. The ties, if you have added them, will now have popped out to the right side.

## ❽ CUTTING OUT THE FOAM

Using a permanent marker, draw around the template onto the foam; cut out the foam. Roll it roughly into thirds and insert through the gap in the cover. As the chair pad is designed to be a tight fit, you will need to manipulate the foam and cover until the foam sits flat. Work around the edge of the chair pad to centre the seam line.

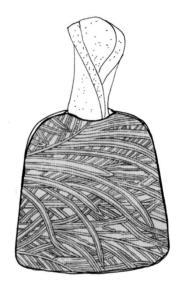

## ❾ ADDING THE MAGNETIC STRIPS

If you are placing the cushions onto metal chairs, use self-adhesive magnetic strips to anchor the pads to the chair. Slip one 10cm length along each side of the foam, with the adhesive side upwards and press into place.

## ❿ ADDING THE FINISHING TOUCHES

Pin the two sides of the opening together and hand stitch to close. Starting at the centre back, pin and then over stitch the bobble edging all the way round the cushion, following the line of the seam. Sew the ends down firmly.

# PATCHWORK PICTURE FRAMES

*With these print-covered picture frames you can create a stunning effect with fabric without even sewing a stitch.*

**YOU WILL NEED**

*for the patchwork frame*
- selection of Liberty Tana Lawn offcuts in prints of your choice (for the green frame we used Speckle in colourway C, May Rose in colourway A and Xanthe Sunbeam in colourway C and for the purple frame we used Ottilia in colourway C, Pointillism in colourway A and Tresco in colourway D)

*for the plain frame*
- rectangle of Liberty Tana Lawn 8cm larger all round than your frame in print of your choice (we used Pointillism in colourway A)

**FOR BOTH STYLE FRAMES YOU WILL NEED**
- old picture frames
- scissors
- PVA adhesive
- sandpaper or sanding block
- old paintbrush
- stencil brush

## PREPARING THE FRAME
To ensure the fabric properly adheres to the existing finish, key the surface by rubbing the whole frame down with sandpaper. A sanding block is especially good for intricate mouldings.

**TRESCO** *is a watercolour study of a selection of flowers, ferns and succulents from the Tresco Abbey Garden.*

## *covering a frame in patchwork pieces*

### ❶ WORKING OUT THE DESIGN

Cut out a selection of rectangles from the Liberty Tana Lawn, each one wide enough to wrap right round the frame with an overlap at each edge. Lay them out over the frame to work out the best arrangement. When you are happy with the design, lift them off one by one and lay them out in the same order on your work surface.

### ❷ STICKING DOWN THE PATCHES

Paint the area of the frame that corresponds to the first patch with a thin coat of PVA adhesive, making sure you cover the top and side edges. If your frame is very ornate, make sure you get glue into all the nooks and crannies. Whilst the glue is still tacky place the fabric, right side up, over the glue-coated area and gently press it down.

❸ To get the fabric to sit right into the frame, use a clean stencil brush to press it down with a dabbing action.

❹ Now turn the frame over, coat the back with glue and stick down the turnings. Continue adding patches until you reach the corners. Fold over and stick down a narrow turning along the overlapping edge of each new patch to give a neat join.

### ❺ ANGLING THE FABRIC ROUND THE CORNERS

Glue the top and sides of the corner area, lay the fabric in place and smooth down the top. Fold the outside corner downwards to check the height of the frame, then cut off a small triangle just outside this point. Snip into the inside corner, right up to the frame. Smooth down the sides.

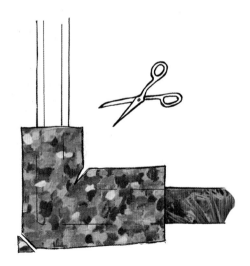

## ❻ NEATENING THE BACK

Paint the reverse of the frame with glue and, stretching the fabric slightly, fold the inside margins to the back. Fold over the margin at the outside corner, then the outside edges. When the glue is dry you can cover up any gaps on the inside corners with small pieces of fabric.

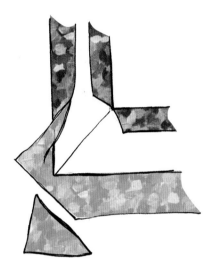

## *covering a frame in a single fabric*

❶ Place the fabric onto a flat surface, right side up, and lay the frame on top. Cut away the fabric from the centre of the frame, leaving a wide enough margin to cover the sides and wrap round to the back. Snip into the corners as before.

❷ Coat the whole frame with a layer of PVA adhesive, diluting it very slightly if it starts to dry out too quickly. Lay the fabric right side up over the frame. Press it down with a stencil brush and finish off as for the patchwork frame.

# COVERED LETTERS

*This simple but effective no-sew project involves manipulating fabric over readily available decoupage bases. So now whatever you want to say, you can spell it in Liberty print.*

**YOU WILL NEED**

- Liberty Tana Lawn in the print of your choice (see note; we used Pinky in colourway A, Saeed in colourway B, Hugo Grenville in colourway D and Tresco in colourway A)
- fleece fabric or wadding (see tip)
- wooden or MDF letter, 1cm deep
- sheet of medium-weight card, the same size as the letter
- 12mm-wide double-sided tape
- staple gun
- glue stick
- scissors

Note: Choose a Liberty Tana Lawn with a small, busy pattern so that any areas where you have to layer the fabric will be less noticeable.

Tip: A base layer of fleece fabric or wadding gives a softly padded look to the finished letter.

**CUTTING OUT**

*from Liberty Tana Lawn*
one rectangle, 4cm larger all round than the letter, for covering
one rectangle, 2cm larger all round than the letter, for the back

*from fleece fabric or wadding*
one rectangle, 4cm larger all round than the letter
(if your letter is deeper than 1cm, allow more fabric to cover)

**PINKY** *was painted by five-year-old pupils from St Bartholomew's School, London.*

## ❶ PREPARING THE CARDBOARD BACKING

Draw around the letter onto the card and cut out around the outline. This will be used to neaten the back of the letter later on.

## ❷ CUTTING THE FLEECE TO SIZE

Run strips of double-sided tape around the back edges of the letter, cutting short lengths to fit around any curves. Peel off the backing papers and place the letter upside down onto the fleece. Trim the fleece so that there is a 3cm margin all round the letter.

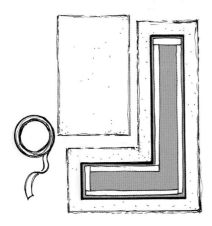

❸ Clip off the surplus fleece at each corner, snipping to within 3mm of the letter and cutting at a 45 degree angle. Cut into the margin at the inside angles so the fleece will wrap neatly around the letter.

## ❹ TURNING BACK THE MARGINS

Starting at the centre of a long edge and working outwards towards the corners, gently pull the edge of the fleece onto the tape and press it down. Fold over the short end, then continue around the letter until all the margins are turned back.

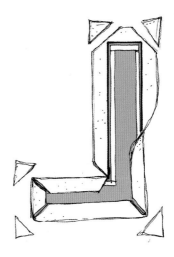

## ❺ COVERING THE LETTER WITH FABRIC

Place the letter, face down, centrally onto the fabric rectangle. Trim the margin to 3cm all round. Fold back the fabric margins and staple them down, again starting in the centre of a straight edge and working towards the corners to keep it smooth.

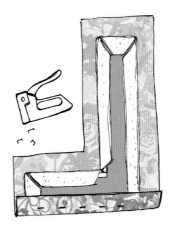

41

## ❻ GOING ROUND CURVES

To cover an outside curve, pleat the fabric slightly and pull it towards the centre of the letter. Position the staples close together. For an inner curve, cover the entire edge with a fabric strip. Clip into the margin at right angles, spacing the cuts at 15mm intervals and snipping to within 3mm of the letter. Coat the back of the fabric with adhesive and stick down over the strip.

## ❼ NEATENING THE CORNERS

When you get to a corner, mitre the surplus fabric for a neat finish. Turn the corner back at an angle, stretching it gently to get a neat edge, and staple down the point. Fold over the margin along the next side of the letter and carry on stapling down.

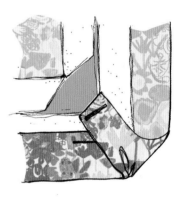

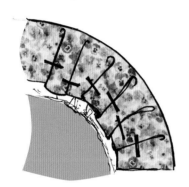

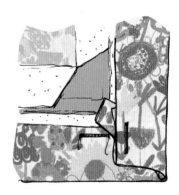

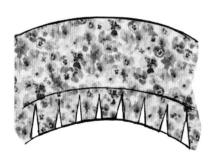

## ❽ DEALING WITH INSIDE ANGLES

You will need to add an extra layer of fabric at each inside angle, or the letter will peep through the cover. Cut a 4cm strip, the same depth as the letter and fix it across the corner with double-sided tape. Snip into the margin at 45 degrees, run a glue stick over reverse side to hold it tightly in place, then staple as before.

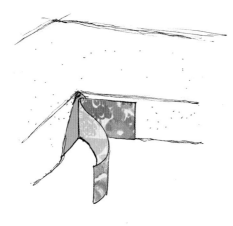

## ❾ COVERING LETTERS WITH HOLES

Cover the inside edge of the corners or curves with fabric strips to conceal the fleece. Cut it deeper than the height of the letter, so it overlaps the back by 1cm. Cover the entire letter with fabric as above, then snip at intervals into the taut fabric across the hole, cutting from the centre outwards. Make a row of cuts along a curve, as in step 6, or snip into any angles as for step 8. Coat the back of the fabric with a glue stick and wrap each section round the fabric covered edge to the wrong side.

## ❿ MAKING THE BACK

Stick lengths of double-sided tape along each edge of the card letter. Lay out the fabric with the right side facing downwards and position the card letter on top, the right side up. Trim the fabric so that there is a 15mm margin all round the edges of the letter. Trim off the surplus fabric across each corner, cutting to within 3mm of the card and snip into the margins along any curves and inside angles. Peel the protective backing paper from the double-sided tape, then fold back the fabric margins and press them onto the adhesive strips.

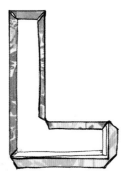

⓫ Cover the entire back with a layer of double-sided tape. Take off the backing paper and press it firmly in place onto the reverse of the wooden letter.

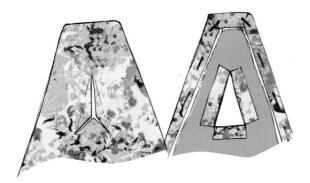

# FABRIC BELT

*Customise an otherwise plain rain
mac or other coat with a Liberty print belt
and covered buttons (see page 47); a simple
way to update an outfit each season.*

**YOU WILL NEED**

- 112 x 20cm Liberty Lifestyle craft fabric in print of your choice (we used Newbury in colourway A)
- 90 x 20cm medium-weight black cotton fabric, for the backing
- air-erasable pen or sharp pencil
- black sewing thread
- large safety pin
- belt buckle (without a prong) to fit 6cm belt

### ❶ PREPARING THE FABRIC STRIPS

Cut out two 8cm-wide strips of Liberty Lifestyle craft fabric, one 110cm and the other 65cm, carefully matching the repeat. Join them together as in step 1 of the dog lead on page 48 so that you have a 173cm long strip. Cut and join the black fabric so that you have a 173 x 8cm backing strip.

### ❷ MARKING THE CURVED END

Using a saucer or small plate as your guide, mark a curved line across one end of the main fabric strip. Draw onto the wrong side of the fabric with an air-erasable pen or sharp pencil.

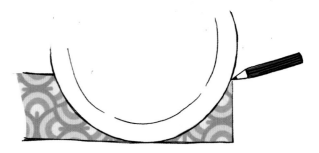

**NEWBURY** *is based on a 1965 design by Agnes Roberts for Liberty. It was printed at Liberty's Merton Abbey Print Works on cotton in 1966.*

### ❸ JOINING THE TWO HALVES TOGETHER

With the right sides facing, pin the two sides of the belt together. Starting at the centre of one long edge, machine stitch all the way around, 1cm from the edge. Follow the curved line carefully to round off the corner and finish the stitch line 10cm from the starting point. Press back the 1cm seam allowance on each side of the gap.

### ❹ TRIMMING THE SEAM ALLOWANCE

Trim the seam allowance along the curve down to 5mm. Snip a sharply angled triangle from each side of the point, then snip a series of little triangles along the curve. Cut to within 2mm of the seam line and space them about 5mm apart. Clip a shallow arrowhead shape from the two corners at the other end.

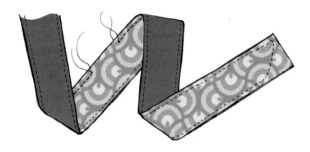

### ❺ TURNING THROUGH

Fix a large safety pin to one end of the belt. Gently feed it between the two layers of fabric towards the centre and out of the gap. Do the same at the other end, then ease out the seams and shape the corners with the point of a pencil. Press the edges lightly.

### ❻ TOP STITCHING THE EDGE

Tack the two sides of the gap together. Using black thread, machine stitch all the way around the belt, 3mm from the edge.

### ❼ SEWING ON THE BUCKLE

Slide the buckle onto the straight end of the belt, then fold back and tack a 5cm turning. Sew it down with two lines of machine stitching, 5mm from the end.

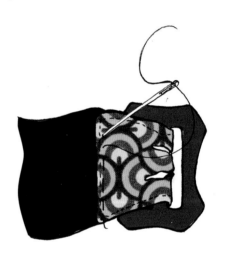

# COVERED BUTTONS

*Covering buttons is a useful technique
for anyone to have in their sewing
repertoire, as it's a speedy yet impactful
way to customise any garment.*

**YOU WILL NEED**

- self-cover buttons – the same size and number as on your coat or garment
- Liberty Lifestyle craft fabric in print of your choice (we used Newbury in colourway A) – allow approximately 10 x 10cm for each button, depending on the size of the pattern
- tracing paper
- air-erasable pen
- black sewing thread
- sewing kit

**CUTTING OUT**

Cut out a circle of tracing paper 15mm wider all round than your button, or cut round the relevant printed circle on the button packaging and use the main card as a window template. Lay out the fabric right side up and centre the template over a pleasing part of the design. Draw round the template with an air-erasable pen and cut around the outline. Make sure that all the buttons use the same pattern area so you will have a matching set.

**❶ GATHERING THE FABRIC**

Using a double length of thread, sew a line of small running stitches around the circle, 5mm from the edge. Leave long tails at the beginning and end to make the gathering easier.

**❷ INSERTING THE BUTTON FRONT**

Pull up the two tails until the fabric is loosely gathered, then insert the button front. Pull the threads up tightly. Check that the fabric pattern is still centred and that the button loop is horizontal, then knot the threads securely. Trim the ends.

**❸ FIXING ON THE BACK**

Check that the gathers are evenly distributed, then press the button back firmly in place to enclose the raw edges.

# DOG LEAD

*With a small amount of Liberty print fabric and by sewing just a few straight seams, you ensure that you and your faithful canine companion are fully coordinated with matching dog lead, belt and buttons.*

**YOU WILL NEED**

- 110 x 15cm Liberty Lifestyle craft fabric in print of your choice for main fabric (we used Newbury in colourway A) – if you need to match up a larger pattern, allow more depth
- 130 x 12cm medium-weight cotton fabric, for backing fabric
- 2cm-wide fusible hem tape
- metal dog lead clip
- matching sewing thread
- sewing machine
- sewing kit

**MEASURING UP**
To find the length of the strips, measure your dog's existing lead from end to end, then add another 27cm for the handle loop and clip turn-back.

**❶ PREPARING THE FABRIC STRIPS**
Cut the main fabric into two matching 4.5cm strips. With right sides facing, join the ends together with a 1cm seam, lining up the repeat if possible. Press the seam open. Trim the strip to the right length for your dog's lead. Cut two 5cm strips from the backing fabric, then join and trim them in the same way.

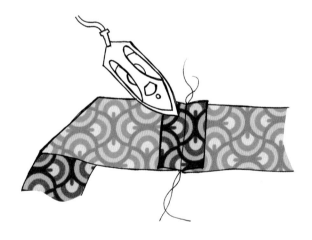

## ② PRESSING THE EDGES

Press under a 1cm turning along each edge of both strips.

## ③ FUSING THE STRIPS

Place the backing strip on your ironing board with the right side facing downwards. Unroll the fusible hem tape and position it centrally over the strip. Trim to length. Now lay the main fabric strip, with the right side upwards, centrally on top so that an equal margin of backing fabric peeps out at both sides.

④ The fusible hem tape is now sandwiched between the two strips. Following the manufacturer's instructions, fuse the layers together, taking care to move the iron in an 'up and down' pressing way to keep strips in the right position.

## ⑤ SEWING THE STRIPS TOGETHER

Thread the sewing machine with black thread. Sew the top layer in place by working a line of stitches 2mm from each folded edge.

## ⑥ MAKING THE HANDLE LOOP

Press under a 1.5cm turning at each end. Fold back another 20cm at one end for the loop and tack the first 4cm to the lead. Sew a 3cm rectangle at the end, then reinforce this by working two diagonal lines from corner to corner.

## ⑦ ATTACHING THE CLIP

Slide the clip onto the lead so that it lies 4cm in from the end, then fold over and tack down the end of the lead. Sew down the folded end with a reinforced rectangle, as for the handle loop, stitching as close to the clip as you can.

# HANGING BIRDS

*The Madauri cotton print collection is perfect for these Indian-inspired peacocks. You can stitch each one in a different combination or make a string of matching birds.*

**YOU WILL NEED**

- selection of Liberty Madauri cotton in prints of your choice (we used Indira in colourways 4 and 5, Priya in colourways 2 and 8, Tehzeeb in colourways 3 and 6, and Zai in colourways 1 and 7)
- matching sewing thread
- tailor's chalk or air-erasable pen
- safety standard polyester toy stuffing
- 2m of 2mm-wide waxed cord
- five 20mm and one 15mm diameter beads
- large upholstery needle
- sewing kit
- sewing machine

**TEMPLATES**

Copy the template on page 155, enlarging it by 220% for bird 1, 200% for bird 2, 160% for bird 3, 140% for bird 4 and 120% for bird 5. Cut neatly around the outlines and number each piece.

**CUTTING OUT**

*from Liberty Madauri cotton*

| | |
|---|---|
| bird 1 tail | one 40 x 23cm rectangle |
| bird 2 tail | one 35 x 20cm rectangle |
| bird 3 tail | one 30 x 18cm rectangle |
| bird 4 tail | one 25 x 14cm rectangle |
| bird 5 tail | one 20 x 12cm rectangle |

**PRIYA** *is based on a bold one-colour pattern that was designed especially for the Liberty spring/summer 2007 collection.*

51

## ❶ CUTTING OUT THE FIRST SIDE OF THE BODY

The bodies for all five birds are made in the same way. Start by pinning the template to the wrong side of the fabric, draw around the edge and cut out 6mm outside the outline.

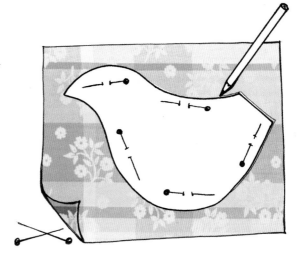

## ❷ MAKING UP AND STUFFING THE BODY

Lining up the stripes, pin the right side of the cut-out body to the right side of the remaining fabric. Stitch along the outline, leaving the tail open between points A and B. Trim the seam allowance back to 3mm. Turn right side out through the opening, then fold and tack a 5mm turning around the opening. Press lightly. Stuff the body, using a pencil to push small amounts of filling down into the head and neck.

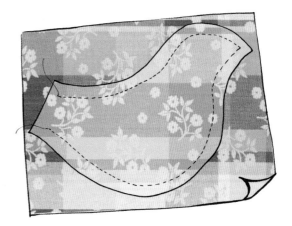

## ❸ STITCHING THE BIRD'S WINGS

The three largest birds have wings. Draw around the template onto the wrong side of the fabric, then cut out 6mm outside the outline and pin to the right side as for the body but without matching the pattern. Stitch all the way round the outline and trim the seam to 3mm. Carefully cut a 2–3cm slit through the centre back and turn the wing right side out through this opening. Reverse the template and make up the second wing in the same way.

### ❹ JOINING THE WINGS TO THE BODY

Stuff the wings lightly with filling, pushing it right to the tips, then hand stitch the opening. Pin the wings to the body, making sure that they are both level and at the same angle, then sew securely in place between points C and D.

### ❺ MAKING AND PRESSING THE FANTAIL

With right sides facing, fold the tail in half widthways. Pin and seam the ends. Turn right side out and press. Mark the centre top with a pin. Starting at this point, fold the fabric into a series of concertina pleats, pressing each one. When you

reach the end, unfold and press the other half from the centre outwards. Make the pleats 2cm wide for the largest bird, and progressively narrower for the others.

### ❻ SEWING THE TAIL TO THE BODY

Refold the tail and stab stitch the bottom ends of the pleats together to make a fan. Slot the tail into the opening. Stitch in place securely, using a thimble to push your needle all the way through the pleats.

### ❼ PUTTING IT ALL TOGETHER

Thread the waxed cord through the upholstery needle and pull it through the centre top of the largest bird's body, close to the seam. Check that the bird hangs straight and alter the position of the cord if not. When it is balanced, pass the second end of the cord through the needle and thread on two beads. Make a knot 10cm from the bird. Pass the needle up through the next bird, check the position and thread on two more beads. Add the other three birds in the same way. Finish off the thread in a loop for hanging.

# BASKET BAG AND SADDLE COVER

·——————•——————·

*This ingenious bag acts as a liner when sat
inside a bicycle basket, but the additional
handles allow you to lift out the bag and
carry it with you. Team the bag with a
matching saddle cover for a sweet ride.*

**YOU WILL NEED**

### for the basket bag
- 50cm Liberty Tana Lawn in prints of
  your choice for outer bag and lining (we
  used Katie and Millie in colourway A
  and Travelling Threads in colourway C)
- 50cm square of plain cotton fabric, for the base
- sheet of paper and pencil
- sheet of corrugated plastic to fit base of basket
- double-sided tape

### for the saddle cover
- 40 x 30cm Liberty Tana Lawn in matching prints
- 40 x 30cm of polyester wadding
- air-erasable pen and clear ruler

**FOR BICYCLE BAG AND SADDLE COVER YOU WILL NEED**
- 1m of 2cm-wide bias binding each for bag and saddle
- 1m of 6mm-wide elastic each for bag and saddle
- matching sewing thread
- sewing machine
- sewing kit
- elastic threader or safety pin

**CUTTING OUT**

### from Liberty Tana Lawn main print
one side piece
handles        two 40 x 15cm rectangles

### from Liberty Tana Lawn lining print
one side piece

### from plain cotton fabric
two bases

### from plastic
one base

**MEASURING UP**

### for the side piece
width = circumference of basket + 10cm
depth = height of basket + 10cm

### for the base
Trace around the basket base to make a paper
template. Cut out 1cm within the line. The
template must lie 1cm inside the basket edge,
so trim it accordingly. Fold in four and mark
the quarter sections with notches.

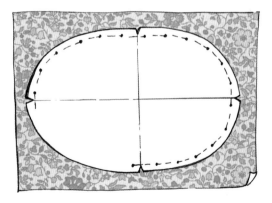

## ① PREPARING THE SIDE PIECE

Fold the main fabric side piece in half widthways, then in half again. Mark the quarter sections by snipping 5mm notches into the lower edge, at the end of each fold. With right sides facing, pin the short edges together and machine stitch with a ιcm seam. Press the seam open.

## ② SEWING THE GATHERING STITCHES

Using a double length of thread, sew four lines of 5mm running stitches between the notches about 8mm from the lower edge. Leave long tails at the end of each row of stitches.

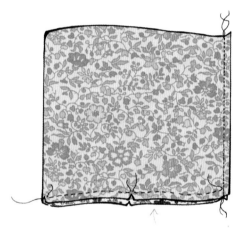

## ③ JOINING THE BASE

With the right side facing inwards, pin the lower edge of the seam to the notch on the top edge of a plain fabric base. Match up and pin the other notches.

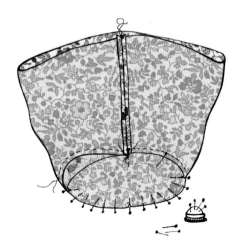

## ④ 

Draw up the first gathering thread so that the edge of the side piece fits exactly along the first quarter of the base. Pin the two together, then do the same with the other three quarter sections. Tack, then machine stitch with a ιcm seam.

## ⑤ 

Turn the bag right side out and place the plastic base inside. Keep it in place with two strips of double-sided tape.

## ⑥ MAKING UP THE BAG

Make up the lining by repeating steps ι to 4 with the lining fabric side piece and plain fabric base. Slip it inside the outer bag, matching the seams and pin the two together along the bottom edge.

## ⑦ 

Work a round of small running stitches close to the plastic.

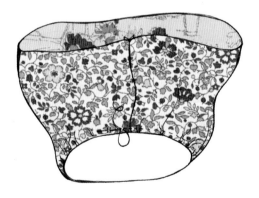

## ❽ BINDING THE OPENING

Pin and tack the top edges of the inner and outer bags together. Fold the bias binding in half and slot it over the top edges, starting close to the seam line. Pin the binding in place all round the opening, then trim the end. Machine stitch 2mm from the edge to make a channel for the elastic, leaving the last 2cm unstitched.

## ❿ ADDING THE HANDLES

Pin the first handle to the bag so that both inside edges lie 6cm from the seam and the ends are 3cm down from the top edge. Tack, then machine stitch in place below the binding with a rectangle crossed by two diagonal lines. Add the second handle to the other side in the corresponding place.

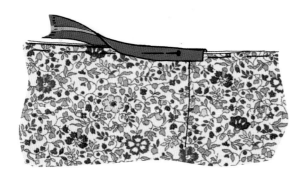

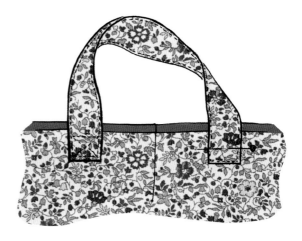

## ❾ MAKING THE HANDLES

Press each handle in half lengthways with the wrong side inwards. Unfold and press over the long edges to meet the centre crease. Press over a 1cm turning at each end. Refold the crease, press once again and tack the edges together. Top stitch round all four edges of the handle.

## ⓫ THREADING THE ELASTIC

Thread the elastic through a bodkin or elastic threader. Ease it through the opening and feed the bodkin all the way around the binding and out again. Pull up the ends slightly and slip the bag over the basket – the top edge should fit snugly but still be easy to remove. Check the fit and sew the two ends securely together. Trim, push the join back through the opening and neaten the loose end of binding.

# SADDLE COVER

*Lightly padded for a more comfortable ride, this saddle cover is reversible so offers a choice of two different prints. A bicycle is simply underdressed without one.*

**CUTTING OUT**
Cut one saddle cover from main and lining fabrics, and from wadding. Trim 1cm all round from the wadding.

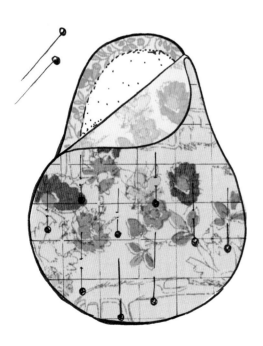

**TEMPLATE**
Copy the template on page 150, enlarging it by 200%.

### ❶ MARKING THE QUILTING LINES
Fold one of the fabric saddle pieces in half lengthways to find the centre. Draw along this line using a clear ruler and an air-erasable pen. Add more parallel lines on each side, spacing them 3cm apart, then draw another set of lines across them, also 3cm apart, to make a square grid.

### ❷ WORKING THE QUILTING
Place the main fabric saddle piece face downwards and centre the wadding on top of it. Position the lining fabric piece on top, right side up, matching the edges carefully. Pin all three layers together, between the vertical lines.

❸ Machine stitch along each of the vertical lines, then remove the pins and machine stitch along the horizontal lines.

### ❹ FINISHING OFF
Neaten the edge with bias binding and add the elastic as for steps 8 and 11 of the bicycle basket bag. Pull up the elastic tightly enough to make the cover a secure fit around the bicycle saddle.

# CAFETIERE COVER AND COASTERS

*Add a shot of colour to the breakfast table with a padded cafetière cosy. By using the same method, you can make a set of coordinating coasters.*

**YOU WILL NEED**

- 90 x 20cm Liberty Tana Lawn in print of your choice (we used Farhad in colourway D)
- 90 x 20cm quilt wadding
- 90 x 20cm plain cotton fabric, for backing
- 4m of 12mm-wide bias binding in a complementary colour
- two 2cm velcro circles
- two 2cm buttons
- matching sewing thread
- dressmaker's squared paper
- sewing machine
- sewing kit

- If you only want to make the cafetière cover, you will need 35 x 20cm each of Liberty Tana Lawn, wadding and backing.

**MEASURING UP**

The cover is designed for a standard 8 cup or 1 litre cafetière. Copy the template on page 151, enlarging it by 200%. Cut out the paper pattern and check the size of the cover against your cafetière before you start sewing. You can then adjust the height or width if necessary.

**TEMPLATES**

Copy the templates on page 151 for the cafetière cover and tabs, enlarging them by 200%.

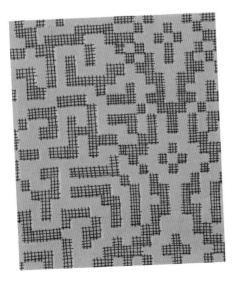

**FARHAD** *was inspired by Art Nouveau repeats and mazes of stately gardens in Vienna. The design captures motifs from both art and nature.*

### ❸ QUILTING THE LAYERS

Thread the machine with matching sewing thread. Starting parallel to the right edge sew a series of vertical lines, 8mm apart, across the entire surface. Keep the right hand edge of the presser foot lined up with the previous row of stitches so that the lines are spaced regularly. Start each row from the top edge to prevent the fabric puckering.

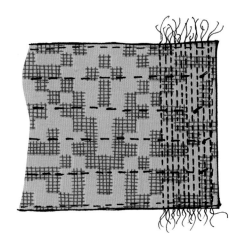

### ❶ LAYERING THE FABRICS

Spread the wadding across the plain fabric and place the Liberty Tana Lawn on top, with the right side facing upwards. Match up the corners and pin all three layers together around the outside edge.

### ❹ CUTTING OUT THE SHAPES

Using the paper templates, cut out the cafetière cover and two tabs from the quilted fabric. Then cut four 14cm squares with gently rounded corners for the set of coasters.

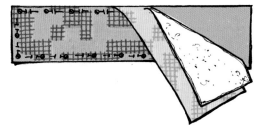

### ❷ WORKING THE TACKING

Using a contrasting thread, tack around all four edges. Now sew four rows of tacking stitches, about 4cm apart, along the width. This will stop the fabrics from sliding about when they are being quilted.

## ❺ BINDING THE EDGES

Open out one end of the binding and turn back the first 1cm. Re-fold the creases. With right sides facing and raw edges matching, pin this end to the left edge of the cafetière cover, about 5cm up from the bottom corner. Tack the binding to the cover, gently stretching the raw edge to fit around the curves. Leave a 1cm overlap at the end and trim.

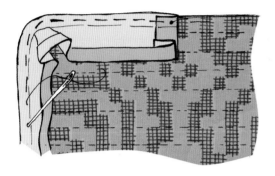

❻ Machine stitch 4mm from the edge, slowing right down at the corners for accuracy. Turn the binding to the wrong side and slip stitch the folded edge to the back of the cover. Bind the tabs and the coasters in the same way.

## ❼ ADDING THE VELCRO AND BUTTONS

Stick the hooked side of the velcro dots to the wrong side of the tabs. Hand or machine stitch them in place, taking care not to catch the binding. Sew the buttons securely to the right side, directly above the dots.

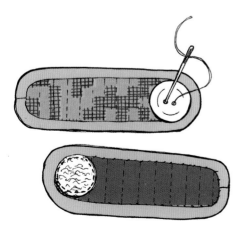

## ❽ SEWING THE TABS TO THE COVER

With the right sides facing downwards, pin the plain ends of the tabs to the left edge of the cover, so that they overlap by 4cm. Wrap the cover around your cafetière and slip the tabs through the handle. Adjust the positions if you need to, then tack the tabs in place. Machine stitch them down from the right side, sewing to within 3mm of the binding.

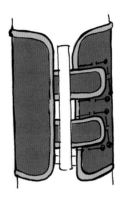

## ❾ POSITIONING THE VELCRO

Put the cover back on the cafetière, this time with the right side outwards. Pin the tabs to the right edge, so that the cover fits snugly. Mark the position of each one with three more pins, then take out the first pins. Stick the looped sides of the velcro dots in place between the pins, stitch them down securely.

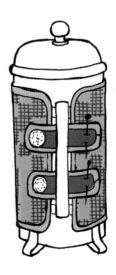

# DRUM LAMPSHADE

*A minimal amount of fabric can provide maximum impact when used to cover a simple drum lampshade. When light passes through the fabric, Liberty prints take on a luminous quality.*

- Liberty Tana Lawn in three different prints and colourways of your choice.
- 140 x 20cm of main print 1 (we used Scilly Flora in colourway B)
- 140 x 10cm of complementary print 2 (we used Scilly Flora in colourway C)
- 140 x 15cm of complementary print 3 (we used Jugenstil in colourway C)
- 1cm-wide double-sided tape
- matching sewing thread
- sewing kit
- plain cardboard drum lampshade
- 25cm high, 40cm diameter with a circumference of 125cm

**MEASURING UP**

| print 1 | 128 x 6cm |
| | 128 x 11cm |
| print 2 | 128 x 8cm |
| print 3 | 128 x 7cm |
| | 128 x 5cm |

The measurements given above are for this particular lampshade: adjust the size of your fabric strips accordingly to fit a different shape. Add 3cm to the depth of both top and bottom strips and 2cm to the depth of the centre strips. The length of each strip should equal the diameter of your shade, plus an extra 3cm.

**SCILLY FLORA** *is a tropical multi-coloured design that was inspired by the wonderful flora of the Tresco Abbey Garden.*

### ❶ MAKING THE COVER

Press the strips and lay them out in their final order. Pin the top two together, then machine stitch together, leaving a 1cm seam allowance. Press the seam open. Add the remaining three strips in the same way.

### ❷

Trim the side edges so that they are perfectly straight. With right sides facing, tack them together, leaving a 1.5cm seam allowance. Slip the cover over the shade to check the size: it should fit snugly with a 2cm overlap at the top and bottom. Remove the cover and adjust if necessary. Machine stitch the seam and press it open. Turn right side out.

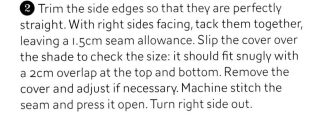

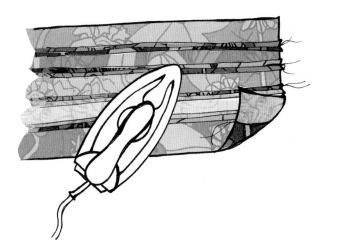

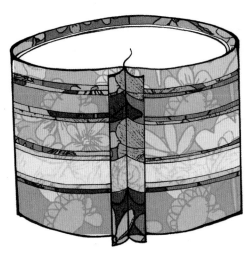

### ❸ FIXING IT IN PLACE

Slip the cover back over the shade so that the seam allowances project equally at the top and bottom edges.

❹ Fix a round of double-sided tape to the inside of the shade, just inside the top edge. Peel off the backing paper. Fold the seam allowance over and press it onto the adhesive. Do the same at the bottom edge.

# CHEVRON QUILT

*If the word 'patchwork' conjures up images of folksy throws then think again. This contemporary, graphic design is deceptively easy to stitch yet is an excellent introduction to core patchwork techniques.*

**YOU WILL NEED**

Liberty Lifestyle craft fabric in five coordinating prints of your choice:
• 112 x 70cm in print 1 (we used Mackintosh in colourway B)
• 112 x 70cm in print 2 (we used Newbury in colourway B)
• 112 x 70cm in print 3 (we used Herbert in colourway B)
• 112 x 60cm in print 4 (we used Wells in colourway B)
• 112 x 110cm in print 5 (we used Lowke in colourway B)
• 3.2m of 112cm-wide white cotton fabric

• 200 x 220cm cotton or bamboo quilt wadding
• 210 x 240cm white double sheet, for the backing
• cutting mat and rotary cutter
• 6 inch quilter's square (see note)
• long ruler
• pencil
• quilter's curved safety pins
• white quilting thread
• matching sewing thread
• sewing machine
• sewing kit

**FINISHED SIZE**
approximately 176.5 x 207cm

**NOTE**
Quilter's squares are marked in inches, not centimetres, so the instructions for cutting out the patches are based on non-metric measurements. The quilt is built up of simple 6in blocks, each made from one white and one blue rectangle. The quickest way to prepare these is by rotary piecing as shown, but alternatively you can join two 6 x 3¼in patches, with a 6mm seam, by either hand or machine to make the block.

**HERBERT** *is based on a Liberty design from the early 1900s, when Liberty was renowned for its iconic Art Nouveau designs.*

# ❶ SEAMING THE STRIPS

Tear off a 10cm deep strip of white fabric and Liberty Lifestyle craft fabric print, ripping them widthways across the fabric. With the right side facing inwards, pin the print fabric to the sheeting. Machine stitch together, leaving a 1cm seam allowance, then press the seam towards the patterned fabric.

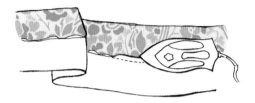

# ❷ CUTTING OUT THE BLOCKS

Place the joined strips, right side up, on a cutting mat. Position the quilter's square on top, with the centre 3in marking directly over the seam line. Carefully cut along each side of the square with a rotary cutter. You will need to make 38 blocks with each of prints 1, 2, 3 and 4, and 29 blocks with print 5. Cut nine 6 x 3¼ in rectangles from print 5 for the top edge and nine from white fabric for the bottom edge.

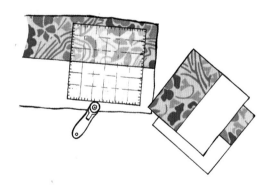

# ❸ LAYING OUT THE BLOCKS

All the blocks are set 'on point' (diagonally). Starting at the top edge, lay out a horizontal row of ten print 5 blocks with the print at the top left. Add the next row of nine print 1 blocks, with the print at the bottom left. Now add ten more print 1 blocks with the print at the top left. Continue adding rows of nine or ten blocks in this way, grading the colours from dark to light: print 2, print 3, then print 4. Repeat the sequence of five zigzag stripes – print 5, print 1, print 2, print 3 and print 4. Add the print 5 rectangles at the top and the white rectangles at the bottom.

# ❹ SEWING ON THE RECTANGLES

Join the rectangles along the top edge of the quilt top to the blocks in the row directly below. With right sides facing, pin the rectangle to the top right edge of the block. Machine stitch with a 6mm seam, then press the seam allowance over the rectangle. Sew the rectangles along the bottom edge of the quilt to the bottom left of the blocks above them.

## ❺ JOINING THE BLOCKS INTO ROWS

The blocks are stitched together in diagonal rows to make four large triangular sections. These are then joined up to make a rectangle. Start at the top right corner of the top triangle. Join the ten blocks that make up the right edge of the triangle, with 6mm seam allowances. Press the seam allowances away from the white fabric. Now join the nine blocks that make up the next row in the same way.

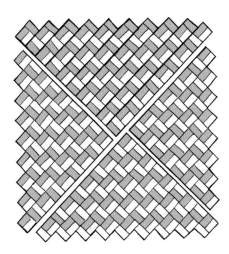

## ❻ JOINING THE ROWS TOGETHER

With right sides facing, pin the two rows together. Match the left edges and insert a pin at each of the points where the seams meet. Machine stitch 6mm from the edge, stopping the seam 6mm from the end of the final rectangle at the outside top edge of the quilt.

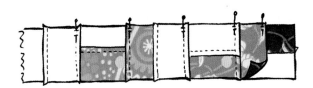

## ❼ PRESSING THE SEAMS

Press back a 6mm turning along the edge of the rectangle and press the long seam allowance downwards, over the first row. This will give you a pre-neatened top edge when you make up the quilt. Join the remaining diagonal rows in the same way until the top triangular section is assembled.

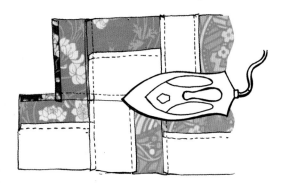

## ❽ ASSEMBLING THE OTHER SECTIONS

Make up the left triangular section, starting with the bottom right row of blocks and matching up the right edge of each row. You can stitch the seams between these rows from edge to edge (without stopping 6mm from the outside edge of the quilt). Join the rows in the right triangular section as for the left triangular section. Then join together the bottom triangular section, neatening the bottom edge in the same way as the top edge.

❾ Join the top section to the left section and the right section to the bottom section. Press the seams to one side, then join the two large triangles to complete the quilt top.

## ❿ TRIMMING THE EDGES

Now trim off the surplus fabric to straighten up the side edges. Place a long ruler along the right edge of the quilt top, in line with the inside corners. Draw a pencil line along the ruler, then continue down to the bottom corner. Do the same on the left edge and cut along both lines.

## ⓫ LAYERING THE QUILT

Press the backing sheet and spread it out over the floor. Spread the wadding centrally on top, then lay the quilt top, right side up, centrally over the two layers. Starting at one edge and working across the quilt, pin the layers together with curved quilter's safety pins. Position them in a regular grid at intervals of about 15cm.

## ⓬ WORKING THE QUILTING

Using white thread, sew lines of short running stitches along the top and bottom edges of each white zigzag, 6mm from the seam lines.

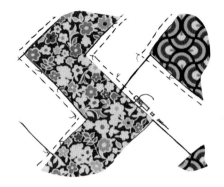

## ⓭ REMOVING THE SURPLUS FABRIC

Tack along the side edges, then trim off the surplus wadding and sheeting in line with the edge of the patchwork. Trim the wadding at the top and bottom in line with the folded edge. Cut away the surplus backing following the zigzag edge, but leaving a 1cm margin as the seam allowance.

## ⓮ NEATENING THE SIDE EDGES

Make a small snip into the margin at each inside corner. Tack the backing to the patchwork, turning the seam allowance inwards as you go, so the two folded edges match exactly. Slip stitch the edges together using dark sewing thread.

## ⓯ BINDING THE SIDE EDGES

Cut four 112 x 5cm strips from the remaining print 5. With right sides facing, join the short ends and press the seams open. Bind the side edges as given for the striped throw on page 148.

# TABLE MATS

*Introduce colour and pattern to your
table settings with these roll-up mats.
Slot your cutlery neatly into the integral
pockets with a contrast-bound edge.*

**YOU WILL NEED**

### for each mat
- 60 x 40cm Liberty Tana Lawn in two complementary prints of your choice (we used Mitsi in colourway B and Glenjade in colourway N)
- 60 x 40cm medium-weight iron-on interfacing
- matching sewing thread
- sewing machine
- sewing kit

**PREPARING THE FABRIC**

Decide which fabric will be uppermost and iron the interfacing to the wrong side of it.

**CUTTING OUT**

Use a rotary cutter, quilter's square and cutting mat for accuracy, or make a template from dressmaker's squared paper.

### from each Liberty Tana Lawn print
for each mat        one 45 x 30cm rectangle
for each pocket     one 8 x 16cm rectangle

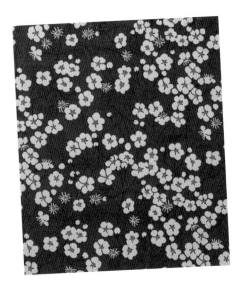

**MITSI** *is based on a design created by the Liberty studio during the
1950s. With its Japanese-style cherry blossom, it plays on Liberty's history.*

## ❷ CLIPPING THE CORNERS

At each corner, measure and mark two points, each 1cm from the corner and draw a line between them. Snip along this line. This may cut into the stitches; don't worry as any gap will be folded into the border.

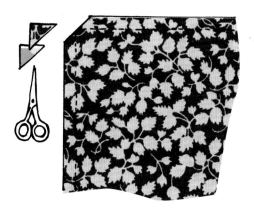

## ❶ JOINING THE TWO LAYERS

Pin the two rectangles together with the right sides facing outwards. Machine stitch around the outside edge leaving a 1cm seam allowance. Trim the seam allowance back to 5mm.

## ❸ TURNING THE EDGES

With the stiffened fabric uppermost, fold over and press a 5mm turning along each edge, using the tip of the iron. Repeat so that you have a double 5mm hem all round and the raw edges are concealed.

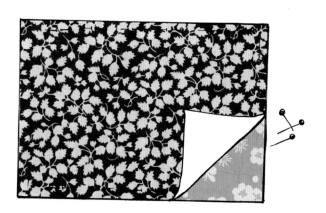

### ❹ SEWING DOWN THE HEM

Using a matching thread, machine stitch the hem down, stitching midway along the turning. The narrow pressed hem should stay in place, so won't need any pins or tacking.

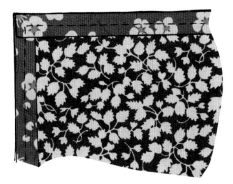

### ❺ MAKING THE POCKET

Pin the two pockets together with right sides facing and machine stitch with a 5mm seam allowance, leaving a 5cm space in the centre of one long edge. Press back the seam allowance on either side of this gap. Clip the corners to lessen the bulk and turn right side out.

❻ Ease out the right angles and press lightly. Turn over the top 4cm to make a cuff and press down this fold.

### ❼ SEWING ON THE POCKET

Position the pocket 2cm up from the bottom edge and 2cm in from the right edge. Pin, then machine stitch 3mm from the edges, remembering to keep the top open for the cutlery. Reinforce both ends of the seam to keep the pocket securely in place.

# 'LIBBY' DOLL

*Every girl adores a Liberty print outfit, and Libby the doll is no different. Because of the small parts, like the shoes, this toy is not suitable for a child under 4 years.*

**YOU WILL NEED**

- 50 x 30cm cream linen fabric
- 100g safety standard polyester toy filling
- stranded cotton embroidery thread in black and pink, for the eyes and mouth
- small ball of brown wool yarn, for the hair
- elasticated hair band, for the hair
- selection of remnants of Liberty Tana Lawn in an assortment of different prints
- 7cm x 5mm strip of velcro
- 30cm square felt
- 12 x 5cm fusible bonding web
- 3 small buttons
- matching sewing thread
- sewing machine
- sewing kit
- 20cm square of card
- knitting needle
- tapestry needle

**TEMPLATES**

Copy the templates on page 152, enlarging them by 200% and cut out the body, arm, leg, bodice, jacket and shoe pattern pieces.

**CUTTING OUT**

### from cream linen fabric
FOR THE DOLL
two bodies
two legs, cut on fold
two arms, cut on fold

### from assorted Liberty Tana Lawn
FOR THE DRESS BODICE
two 25 x 20cm rectangles
FOR THE DRESS SKIRT
two 6 x 50cm rectangles
two 8 x 50cm rectangles
two 10 x 50cm rectangles
two 12 x 50cm rectangles
FOR THE DRESS SASH
one 8 x 40cm strip

### from felt
FOR THE JACKET
two 25 x 15cm rectangles
FOR THE SHOES
one 5 x 12cm rectangle. Fuse the felt to a scrap of Liberty Tana Lawn using bonding web, following the manufacturer's instructions.

*making the doll*

## ❶ MAKING UP THE HEAD AND BODY

Referring to the template, mark the features, hairline and points A, B and C on one of the body pieces. With right sides together, pin and tack both body pieces together. Machine stitch twice around the head and shoulders from points A to A, to reinforce the seam line. Stitch both side edges between points B and C, working a few reverse stitches at each end to secure the seams.

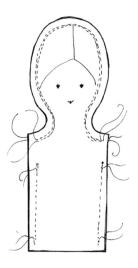

## ❷ FINISHING OFF THE SEAMS

Trim the seam allowance around the head and shoulders back to 5mm. Clip a row of small triangles into the seam allowance, cutting to within 2mm of the stitch line. Space the notches 5mm apart along the neck curves and 1cm apart around the head. Press back the seam allowance at the side and bottom edges of the body, at both front and back.

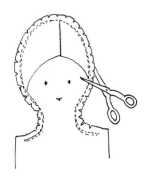

## ❸ SEWING THE LEGS AND ARMS

Re-fold the arms and legs and tack the edges together. Machine stitch these seams, leaving a 1cm seam allowance, once again reinforcing both ends. Trim the seam allowance back to 5mm, tapering it down to 3mm at the narrow ends.

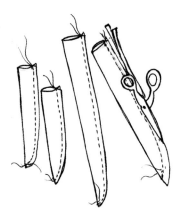

## ❹ TURNING THROUGH

Turn all the parts right side out, using a knitting needle to push the limbs through. Ease out the seams by rolling them between your fingers and thumbs so that the stitches lie at the outside edges.

82

## ❺ STUFFING THE DOLL

Stuff all the doll parts firmly, using the knitting needle to push the toy filling right down into the hands and feet and up through the neck into the head. Make sure that the neck is stuffed well before filling the body, to ensure that the head will stay upright. Tack across the top edge of the arms and legs, with the seam lines at the centre back.

## ❻ ADDING THE LEGS AND ARMS

Slip the top of the legs into the bottom of the body. Pin and tack in place, then hand stitch with matching thread, sewing securely through all the layers. Insert the top of the arms into the side openings, in line with the shoulders. Fix in place as for the legs.

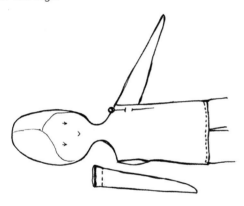

## ❼ EMBROIDERING THE FEATURES

Using black cotton embroidery thread, sew a 4cm vertical black stitch for each eye, with a shorter stitch at a slight angle either side for the eyelashes. Her mouth is a short pink straight stitch caught in the middle with a small stitch to turn it into a smile. Add a little real blusher to give her rosy cheeks.

## ❽ MAKING THE HAIR

Draw a 15cm line along the centre front of the card and wind the wool yarn evenly at right angles to the line until it is covered by the yarn. Cut a length of yarn from the end and thread it through a tapestry needle. Sew a row of backstitches along the centre line: this will be the doll's parting. Cut through the yarn along the centre back of the card.

## ❾ STYLING THE HAIR

Pin the stitched line along the parting and down the centre back of the head. Using matching thread, hand stitch in place along the parting. Stitch the front hair in place either side of the face with a strand of wool and trim to the same length all round. Gather it into a low pony tail and secure with a hair band. Divide this in two just above the band and tuck the loose ends up through the gap.

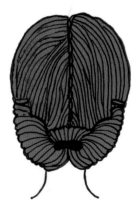

*making the dress*

## ❶ MAKING THE BODICE

Place the two Tana Lawn rectangles together with right sides facing, then pin on the template. Carefully following the edge, machine stitch around the side and top of the paper, leaving the bottom edge open. Cut out, leaving a 5mm seam allowance. Clip into the seam allowance as for the doll's head. Press a 1cm turning around the bottom edge, then turn right side out. Ease out the seams and press lightly.

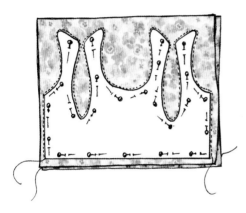

## ❷ MAKING THE SKIRT FRILLS

Pin the four pairs of Tana Lawn rectangles together with right sides facing and sew along the side and bottom edges. Clip the corners, turn right side out and press. Set your machine to the longest straight stitch and sew two rows along each frill, 5mm down from the top edge and 5mm apart, leaving long ends.

## ❸ ASSEMBLING THE SKIRT

Find the two top threads (one from each row of stitching) at one corner of the first rectangle and gently pull them whilst with your other hand gathering up the fabric. When you have gathered half the rectangle, repeat from the other end. Adjust the gathers until the frill measures 20cm wide.

❹ Do the same with the other three frills, then layer them one on top of the other, with the longest frill at the bottom. Tack the top edges of the frills together and zigzag through all the gathers.

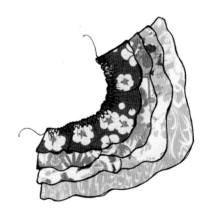

## ❺ JOINING THE SKIRT TO THE BODICE

Slip the zigzagged skirt edge between the front and back layers of the bodice, then pin and tack it in place. Machine stitch through all the layers: this seam doesn't have to be perfect as it will be concealed by the sash.

## ❻ SEWING THE SASH

Fold the Tana Lawn strip in half lengthways with right sides facing. Pin the raw edges together and machine stitch 1cm from the edge. Leave a 5cm gap in the centre of the long edge and angle the seams at the short edges to create points. Press back the seam allowance either side of the opening, trim the corners, turn right side out and press. Slip stitch the opening to close. Hand stitch the sash to the top of the skirt so it conceals the seam line.

## ❼ FINISHING OFF

Separate the two halves of the velcro strip and machine stitch one half to each side of the bodice opening at the back of the dress. Place the dress on the doll, press the velcro strips together to do up the bodice and double knot the shoulder and waist ties.

## *making the flower*

**1** Make a little flower from the remaining felt and fabric, using pinking shears to cut out a 15mm circle. Sew a button in the centre and sew to the doll's hair.

## *making the jacket*

**1** Place the two felt rectangles together and pin on the template. Again following the edge of the paper closely, stitch the shoulder, side and underarm seams. Secure both ends of the stitched lines with a few reverse stitches. Cut out just outside the template, 3mm from the stitch lines, then cut down the centre front of the jacket. Turn right side out.

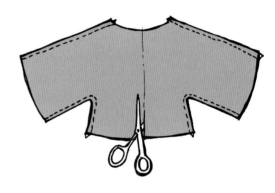

## *making the shoes*

**1** Cut the bonded felt and Tana Lawn into two 6cm squares. Fold one in half, with the felt facing inwards, and pin the template along the fold. Draw around the outline, then machine stitch along the sole. Snip out the semicircle, cut along the instep and trim the seam back to 3mm. Turn right side out, fit onto doll's foot and stitch on securely. Sew a small button to the outside edge. Make the other shoe in the same way.

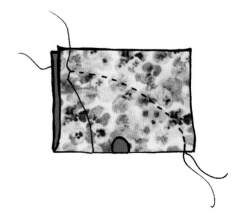

# FLORAL GARLAND

*This impossibly pretty floral garland is not just exceptionally simple to make, it also is an effective way to use up leftover scraps of fabric from other projects.*

- selection of remnants of Liberty Tana Lawn in an assortment of different prints, including a green colourway for the leaves
- fusible bonding web
- one or two buttons for each flower centre
- stranded cotton embroidery thread
- air-erasable pen or chalk pencil
- pinking shears
- sewing thread
- sewing machine
- sewing kit

## TEMPLATES

Copy the templates on page 150, enlarging them by 200%, and cut out the inner and outer flowers, the centre circle and the leaf pattern pieces.

## PREPARING THE FABRIC

The three layers that make up each flower are all double-sided, with a different Liberty Tana Lawn print on the front and back fused together with fusible bonding web. The leaves are also double-sided. To prepare the bonded fabric, choose two different prints of similar size and press a same-shaped piece of fusible bonding web to the wrong side of the first fabric, following the manufacturer's instructions. Peel off the backing paper and iron the adhesive side to the wrong side of the second fabric.

### CUTTING OUT

Draw round the edges of the flower and leaf templates directly onto the double-sided bonded fabric using an air-erasable pen or chalk pencil. Neatly cut out each shape. Use pinking shears to cut out the centre circles and leaves.

### FOR ONE METRE OF GARLAND YOU WILL NEED

*from assorted Liberty Tana Lawn*
four outer flowers
four inner flowers
four centre circles (cut out with pinking shears)
5cm wide strips in various lengths (10–25cm) for the garland string

*from green Liberty Tana Lawn*
three leaves (cut out with pinking shears)

### ❶ ASSEMBLING A FLOWER

Position the inner flower on top of the outer flower so that the petals sit alternately, then place the centre circle in the middle. Using all six strands of embroidery thread, sew them together at the centre point with a few small stitches, then pass the needle through to the back.

❷ Fold the flower into quarters. Stitch three or four times through the tip of the fold to hold the layers together and to give the flower its three-dimensional quality.

### ❸ ADDING THE CENTRE BUTTON

Open out the flower and sew one or two buttons securely to the centre using all six strands of a contrasting embroidery thread.

### ❹ MAKING UP THE GARLAND STRING

With right sides facing, pin two floral strips together at the short ends. Machine stitch leaving a 1cm seam, then press the seams open. Continue adding more strips until you have the required garland length, then press the seams open.

❺ Press the garland string in half lengthways, so that the seams are on the inside, then unfold. Turn and press one long edge inwards so that it lies along the centre crease.

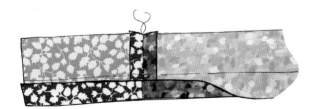

❻ Press a similar turning along the other edge, then refold the centre and press the garland string in half. Sew the folded edges together with a 3mm seam.

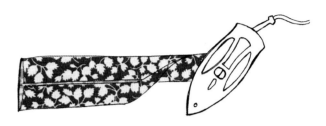

### ❼ PUTTING THE GARLAND TOGETHER

Now decide on the order of the flowers, placing them alongside the garland string at approximately 25cm intervals. Securely hand stitch the folded tip of each flower to the string, using a double length of sewing thread. Tie the leaves to the string in the gaps between the flowers.

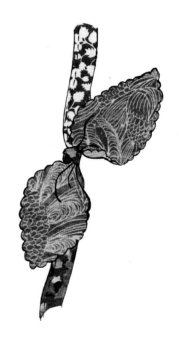

# STORAGE BOLSTER

*Storing your winter duvet can be a bit of a problem, but this beautiful velvet bolster can solve your dilemma and add some glamour to your bedroom.*

**YOU WILL NEED**

- 100cm square Liberty cotton velvet in print of your choice (we used Felix Raison in colourway A)
- 100cm square medium-weight plain cotton fabric
- 2m of 3cm-wide velvet ribbon, for the trim
- 2m of 2cm-wide velvet ribbon, for the ties
- matching sewing thread
- sewing machine
- sewing kit
- large safety pin

**CUTTING OUT**

*from Liberty cotton velvet*
one 92cm square

*from plain cotton fabric*
two 18 x 92cm rectangles
two 22 x 92cm rectangles

The finished length of the stuffed bolster is approximately 135cm and it fits a double bed. Adjust the width of the velvet panel to make it longer or shorter.

## PREPARING THE FABRIC

Neaten all four edges of each piece with an overlock or zigzag stitch.

**FELIX RAISON** *was inspired by a Liberty dress fabric design that was based on an 1850s paisley shawl drawing found in the Liberty archive.*

## ❶ MARKING THE RIBBON CHANNELS

Press under, then unfold, a 5cm turning at one long edge of each 18cm rectangle. These turnings will later form the gathering channels for the ribbon ties.

## ❷ JOINING THE COTTON RECTANGLES

With right sides facing, pin the uncreased long edges of the 18cm rectangles to the 22cm rectangles. Tack together and machine stitch 15mm from the edge. Press the seam allowances open.

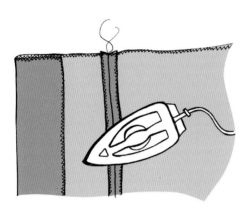

## ❸ ASSEMBLING THE BOLSTER

Pin the other long edges of the 22cm rectangles, with right sides facing, to the side edges of the velvet square. Tack the seams securely with two rows of 1cm stitches to minimise any movement between the fabrics when they are sewn together. Machine stitch 10mm from the edge, sewing both seams from top to bottom. If the velvet now projects below the cotton rectangles, simply trim off the excess fabric and re-neaten the edge.

## ❹ TRIMMING THE SEAMS WITH RIBBON

Press the seams open. To avoid damaging the velvet, press lightly from the wrong side and lay a clean towel over your ironing board to protect the fabric's pile. Cut the 3cm ribbon in half, then pin and securely tack one length centrally over each seam. Using matching thread, machine stitch both edges from top to bottom, to prevent the ribbon from puckering.

## ❺ MAKING UP THE TUBE

Fold the completed cover in half lengthways with the right side inwards. Pin the long edges together, carefully matching the ends of the ribbon and the other two seam lines. Work two lines of tacking as before. Mark a point 9cm from each end, then stitch between these points, taking a 15mm seam allowance. Reinforce both ends of this seam.

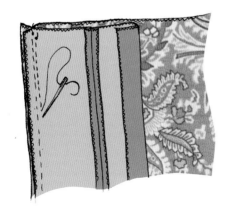

### ❻ PRESSING THE LONG SEAM

Roll up the towel and place it inside the cover to protect the velvet. Gently press the whole seam allowance open with the tip of your iron.

### ❼ MAKING THE RIBBON CHANNELS

Tack down the unstitched seam allowances at each end and machine stitch 5mm from the folds.

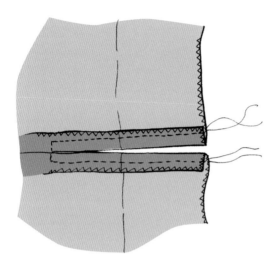

### ❽

Refold the 5cm turnings, then pin and tack the neatened edges in place all around the tube. Starting at the seam line, machine stitch 1cm from the edge. Reinforce the opening by stitching backwards and forwards across the point where the seam meets up.

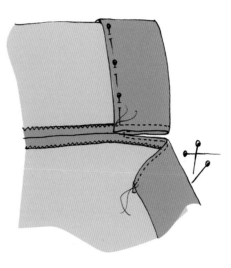

### ❾ THREADING THE RIBBONS THROUGH THE CHANNELS

Turn the bolster right side out. Cut the 2cm ribbon in half and fasten a large safety pin to the end of one length. Feed the pin through the channel, then thread the second length through the other end.

### ❿ STUFFING THE BOLSTER WITH YOUR DUVET

Roll the duvet up tightly from top to bottom. Push one end as far into the bolster as you can, then pull it through from the other end: having a helper will speed up the process. Pull up the ribbons tightly, knot them and tie them with a bow.

# LEAF CUSHIONS

*Appliqué is a quick yet effective technique
for producing decorative effects using fabric.
Graphic shapes that are not too fine, like
this leaf silhouette, work best.*

**LARGE CUSHION**
- 60 x 40cm Liberty Tana Lawn in print of your choice (we used Wiltshire in colourway P)
- 62 x 42cm old gold linen, for the cushion front
- 70 x 45cm black linen, for the cushion back
- 38cm zip
- 60 x 40cm fusible bonding web
- 60 x 40cm cushion pad

**SMALL CUSHION**
- 45 x 30cm Liberty Tana Lawn in print of your choice (we used Lodden in colourway D or Felix and Isabelle in colourway D)
- 47 x 32cm black or olive green linen, for the cushion front
- 55 x 35cm old gold linen, for the cushion back
- 25cm zip
- 45 x 30cm fusible bonding web
- 45 x 30cm cushion pad

**CUTTING OUT**

*from black linen*

| wide back panel | one 53 x 42cm rectangle |
| narrow back panel | one 13 x 42cm strip |

**CUTTING OUT**

*from old gold linen*

| wide back panel | one 40 x 32cm rectangle |
| narrow back panel | one 11 x 32cm strip |

**FOR BOTH SIZE CUSHIONS YOU WILL NEED**
- sharp pencil
- matching sewing thread
- contrasting sewing thread
- sewing machine
- sewing kit

**TEMPLATES**
Copy the templates on page 153, enlarging them by 400% and cut out the small cushion leaves and large cushion leaves pattern pieces.

*The large and small cushions are made in the same way, regardless of size.*

## ❶ CUTTING OUT THE APPLIQUÉ LEAVES

Scale up the appropriate template on page 153 and trace the outline onto the paper side of the fusible bonding web. Roughly cut out and iron the adhesive side onto the back of the floral fabric, following the manufacturer's instructions. Neatly cut out along the pencil line.

## ❸ NEATENING THE EDGES

Set the machine controls to a narrow blanket or zigzag stitch. Using sewing thread to match or contrast with the floral fabric, sew all the way around the outside edge of the leaf motif. Carefully follow the contours to conceal the raw edges.

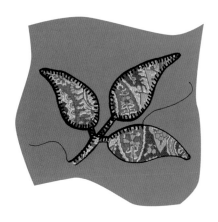

## ❷ FIXING THE LEAVES TO THE CUSHION FRONT

Gently peel off the backing paper and position the leaf across the cushion front. Fuse it in place with a dry iron, using a pressing rather than a gliding action so it doesn't distort.

## ❹ JOINING THE BACK PANELS

Pin one long edge of the narrow strip to one short edge of the wide back panel with right sides facing. Machine stitch 2cm from the edge for 3cm at each end of the seam, securing each one with a few extra stitches at the start and end. Tack the centre of the seam together.

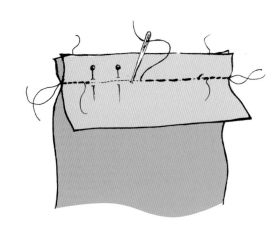

## ❺ ADDING THE ZIP

Press the seam open. Lay the right side of the zip centrally across the seam allowances so that the teeth are in line with the join and tack it securely in place.

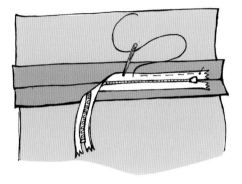

## ❻

Now fit a zipper foot to your machine and thread it with matching sewing thread. Working from the right side, stitch around the zip, 8mm from the join. Carefully unpick the tacking stitches and open the zip.

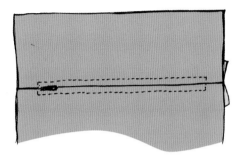

## ❼ MAKING UP THE COVER

Pin the front and back covers with right sides facing and corners matching, then machine stitch all the way round, 10mm from the outside edge. Trim the seam back to 5mm and neaten the raw edges with an overlock or zigzag stitch. Turn the cover right side out and lightly press. Insert the cushion pad and do up the zip.

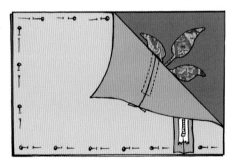

**LODDEN** *is an original William Morris design, first produced by Morris & Co in 1884.*

# EDGED PILLOWCASES

*The fine, high thread count of Liberty
Tana Lawn gives the fabric a luxurious,
silky feel while remaining durable
and so is perfect for a pillowcase.*

### YOU WILL NEED

*for a pair of pillowcases*

- 135cm x 100cm Liberty Tana Lawn in print of your choice for the main fabric (we used May Rose in colourway B)
- 135cm x 100cm Liberty Tana Lawn in print of your choice for the coordinating fabric (we used Saeed in colourway A)
- 110 x 50cm plain white cotton fabric
- dressmaker's squared paper
- matching sewing thread
- sewing machine
- sewing kit

**CUTTING OUT**

To allow for any shrinkage, launder the fabric at 40°C and press well before cutting out.

*from Liberty Tana Lawn main print*

| | |
|---|---|
| main pillowcase | one 135 x 50cm rectangle |
| scallop edging | two 50 x 15cm strips |
| striped border | two 50 x 3.5cm strips |

*from Liberty Tana Lawn coordinating print*

| | |
|---|---|
| main pillowcase | one 135 x 50cm rectangle |
| scallop edging | two 50 x 15cm strips |
| striped border | two 50 x 3.5cm strips |

*from plain white cotton fabric*

| | |
|---|---|
| cuff | two 50 x 35cm rectangles |
| striped border | six 50 x 3.5cm strips |

**TEMPLATE**

Copy the template on page 153, enlarging it by 200%, and cut out the scallop edge pattern piece.

**MAY ROSE** *was hand-drawn from sunflowers to represent the annual
worldwide sunflower planting by the Guerilla Gardeners on 1st May.*

## ❶ MAKING THE SCALLOP EDGING

Place one scallop edging strip of each Tana Lawn together with right sides facing and lay the paper pattern piece centrally on top. Pin it in place, positioning the pins about 2cm in from the edge. Machine stitch slowly along the scallops, carefully following the curved edge of the paper template.

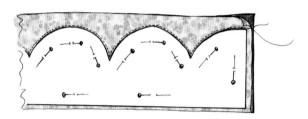

❷ Trim the straight side edges in line with the template, then remove the pins. Trim the seam allowance along the curved scalloped edge down to 3mm. Snip vertically between the curves, cutting right down to 1mm from the stitch line.

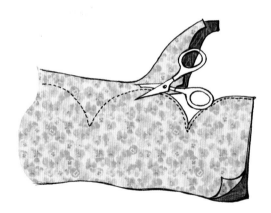

❸ Turn the scalloped edging right side out, ease out the curves using the blunt end of a pencil and lightly press. Tack the straight edges together.

## ❹ SEWING THE STRIPED BORDER

Pin a narrow white strip to the right side of a Tana Lawn strip. Machine stitch, 1cm from the edge. Press the seam allowance so it lies across the Tana Lawn. Join another white strip to the Tana Lawn in the same way, followed by a strip of contrasting Tana Lawn and a third white strip.

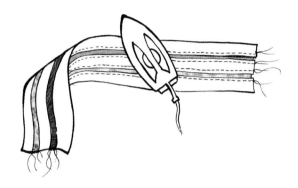

## ❺ ADDING THE CUFF

Press under a 2cm turning along one long edge of the white cuff and lay it out right side up. Place the scalloped edging on top, matching the raw edges and with the light side uppermost. Now place the striped border over the scallops with the dark strip at the top and right side downwards. Pin all three layers together along the top edge and machine stitch taking a 1cm seam allowance. Press the striped border away from the scallops and the cuff.

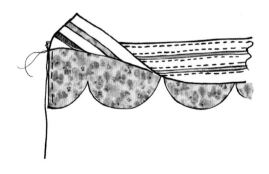

### ❻ JOINING ON THE PILLOWCASE

Trim the selvedge (the woven side edge) from one end of the darker main pillowcase. With right sides facing, pin the striped border to this edge and machine stitch, taking a 1cm seam allowance. Press the seam towards the border.

### ❽ FINISHING OFF

Measure two points, 70cm from the top and bottom corners of the border and mark them with pins. With right sides facing, fold the pillowcase between these points. Pin the top and bottom edges together starting from the pins and working towards the border.

❼ Fold the neatened edge of the cuff over to the wrong side of the pillowcase so that it covers the raw seams. Position the fold so that it overlaps the last seam line by 1cm then pin and tack it down. From the right side, sew the cuff in place by machine stitching along the first white strip, 2mm from the seam line.

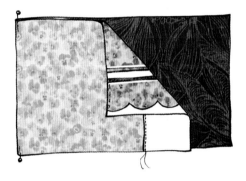

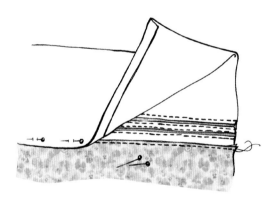

❾ Turn the remaining flap back over the border and pin the top and bottom edges in place. Machine stitch the top and bottom edges leaving a 1.5cm allowance. Trim the seams back to 5mm and neaten with a zigzag or overlocking stitch. Turn right side out, ease out the corners and lightly press. Make up the second pillowcase in the same way from the remaining pieces of fabric.

# SEWING TIDY

*A great way to use up leftovers of furnishing fabric, this portable hanging storage system, with pockets and places for all your sewing notions, means your scissors, needles and pins are always to hand.*

**YOU WILL NEED**

- 110 x 80cm cream cotton drill fabric
- 130 x 20cm Liberty Linen Union in print of your choice (we used September Roslynd in colourway A)
- 30cm matching bias binding
- 20 x 5cm felt
- 20cm narrow lace
- small amount of polyester toy filling
- wooden coat hanger
- sharp pencil
- dressmaker's squared paper
- matching sewing thread
- sewing machine
- sewing kit

**CUTTING OUT**

### from cotton drill fabric

| | |
|---|---|
| front panel | one 50 x 60cm rectangle |
| back panel | one 50 x 60cm rectangle |
| strawberry pincushion | |

### from Liberty Linen Union

pleated pocket
large divided pocket
small divided pocket
large scissor pocket
small scissor pocket
knitting needle pocket

### from felt

needlebook cover
needlebook pages
strawberry hull

**TEMPLATES**

Copy the templates on page 157, enlarging the pleat pocket template by 400% and all the other templates by 200%.

**SEPTEMBER ROSLYND** *is a hand-drawn Art Nouveau graphic design from a dress fabric for the Liberty autumn/winter 2009 collection.*

# ❶ SHAPING THE FRONT AND BACK PANELS

Mark the centre top of one panel. Position the coat hanger across this edge so that the hook is in line with the mark and draw along the upper edge of the hanger. Extend the curve out to the side edges, then neatly cut along the marked line. Use this piece as a template to shape the second panel.

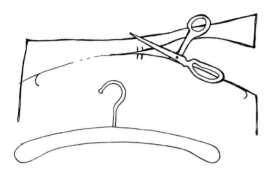

# ❷ MAKING THE PLEATED POCKET

Press under a 12mm turning along the side and bottom edges of the pocket, and make a double 12mm hem along the top edge. Insert pins into the top and bottom edges to mark the fold lines, at 2.5cm and 10cm intervals, following the broken lines marked on the template. Fold and press each line in turn to create four inverted pleats.

# ❸

Pin the pleats together and position the pocket centrally on the front panel, 5cm up from the bottom edge. Pin and tack the side edges, then machine stitch 3mm from the fold. Now tack down the bottom edge and stitch through all the layers, 3mm from the fold. Divide up the pockets by hand stitching a vertical line down the centre of each inverted pleat. If you prefer, you can sew this and the other pockets on by hand with small slip stitches.

# ❹ ADDING THE SMALL POCKETS

Bind the top edge of all five pockets with bias binding (see page 11 for how to do this). Press back a 1cm turning along the bottom edge of each pocket, then press a 1cm turning along the side edges. Fold the corners down and press them too, so that they don't project above the top edge. Press the divided pockets in half and then into quarters to mark the stitch lines.

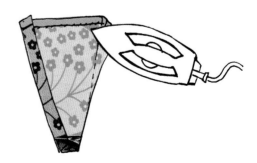

**5** Following the photograph as a guide, pin the knitting needle pocket and the large scissor pocket above and to the left of the pleated pocket and the small scissor pocket to the right.

**6** Position the divided pockets in the top right half, with the right edges in line with the pleated pocket. Machine stitch down, 3mm from the folds, then sew along the crease lines on the divided pockets.

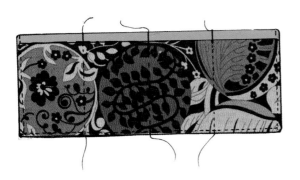

## **7** SEWING THE STRAWBERRY
Join the two straight edges with a 6mm seam. Trim a small triangle from the tip, then turn right side out. Sew small running stitches around the top edge and stuff firmly with toy filling. Draw up the thread and securely fasten off. Cut a 10cm length of lace and fold it in half. Sew the ends together and thread on the hull. Stitch the ends of the lace to the top of the strawberry and sew down the tips of the hull.

## **8** ASSEMBLING THE NEEDLEBOOK
Fold the remaining lace in half and sew the ends to the centre top edge of the cover. Pin the felt page to the cover and hand stitch the left edge. Fold the book in half and work a few stitches through the spine to keep the book flat. Stitch the top of both lace loops to the front panel.

## **9** PUTTING IT ALL TOGETHER
With right sides facing, pin the front and back panels together. Machine stitch 15mm from the edge along the side and top edges, leaving a 1cm gap at the centre top, where marked. Press the seam open, then press a 1cm turning along both bottom edges. Turn right side out. Insert the coat hanger, pushing the hook up through the gap. Pin and tack the front to the back along the bottom edge and sew together by hand or machine.

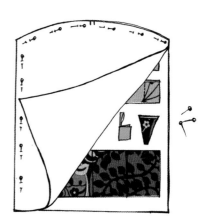

# GRAFFITI TABLE RUNNER

● *This update on the classic table runner combines traditional sewing with unconventional spray paint. The double discs of Liberty Tana Lawn are juxtaposed by vintage doilies coloured neon pink.*

**YOU WILL NEED**

- 50cm-wide natural linen runner, 30cm longer at each end than your table
- 40 x 30cm Liberty Tana Lawn in print of your choice for the main fabric (we used Mauverina in colourway E)
- 60 x 25cm Liberty Tana Lawn in print of your choice for the contrasting fabric (we used Mauvey in colourway B)
- 80 x 35cm pale blue cotton
- 60 x 30cm grey cotton
- bright fuchsia sewing thread
- 2m of 45cm-wide fusible bonding web
- selection of old lace and crochet doilies
- neon pink spray paint
- air-erasable pen or tailor's chalk
- sewing machine
- sewing kit

## ❶ STENCILLING THE DOILIES

Lay the linen runner out on a flat surface outdoors or in a well-ventilated room. Protect any floor coverings or nearby furniture with newspaper. Place a lace or crochet doily halfway over one end and spray the bottom 8cm with neon paint, holding the can 20cm from the linen and spraying evenly along the hem. Repeat at the other end.

**MAUVEY** *is based on a mixture of Mallow shrub flowers and sequins, designed by Liberty's design studio for spring/summer 2008. It has been re-scaled and recoloured for the Classic Tana Lawn range.*

115

**❷** Position three other doilies across the runner, 1m and 50cm in from each end and one towards the centre, close to the side edge. Spray over them in the same way. When the paint is dry, remove the doilies to reveal the beautiful pattern left on the fabric.

### ❸ DRAWING UP THE FABRIC CIRCLES

The easiest way to make a perfect circle is to draw round a plate or saucer, so sort through your kitchen cupboard to find a good selection of crockery in various sizes. These seven circles are 33cm, 28cm, 27cm, 22cm, 21cm, 20cm, 16cm and 15cm in diameter, but this is a very individual project and each runner will be different.

**❹** Position all the plates (except the 28cm and 21cm ones) upside down on the paper side of the fusible bonding web in turn and draw around the outside edge with a pencil. Write the size of the plate on the paper, so you will be able to identify the circles. Leave about 1cm round each outline.

**❺** Cut out each bonding web circle roughly and iron them onto the wrong side of the Liberty Tana Lawn fabrics following the manufacturer's instructions. Press the 27cm and 15cm circles to the main print; the 22cm, 20cm and 16cm circles to the contrasting print; the 33cm circle to the pale blue cotton. Now cut each circle out accurately around the pencil line.

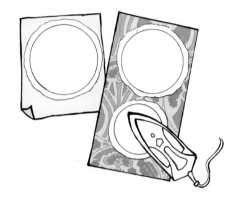

### ❻ MAKING THE DOUBLE-SIDED CIRCLES

The small pale blue and the grey circles that project over the edge of the runner are double-sided. Cut two 24cm squares from the remaining pale blue fabric and iron a 24cm square of fusible bonding web to one of them. Peel off the backing paper. Draw round the 21cm plate onto the other square using an air-erasable pen or tailor's chalk. Pin the two squares together with right sides facing and machine stitch around the line, leaving about 10cm unstitched for turning through.

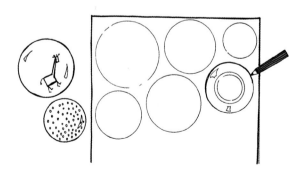

**7** Trim away the surplus fabric, leaving a 2mm seam allowance and cutting straight across the gap. Turn right side out through the gap, ease out the seam and press. As you press you will activate the fusible bonding web's adhesive and the two sides of the circle will fuse together. Do the same with the grey fabric, cutting it into two 32cm squares and drawing round the 28cm plate.

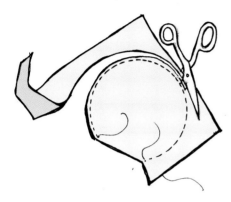

## **8** ARRANGING THE CIRCLES

Spread the linen runner across your table, making sure there is an equal overhang at each end. Position the double-sided circles so that they project beyond the side edges and arrange the other circles until you have decided on the layout. Be sure to cover up to straight, open edge of each double-sided circle with another overlapping circle. Take a picture for reference.

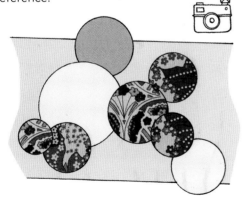

**9** Iron the bonding web to the parts of the double-sided circles that will lie over the linen and peel off the backing paper.

## **10** TRIMMING THE OVERLAPS

To ensure the overlapping layers lie flat you will need to cut away part of each lower circle. To do this, draw round the uppermost circles with an air-erasable pen or tailor's chalk onto the circles below. Cut away the marked segments from the underlying circles.

## **11** PRESSING THE CIRCLES IN PLACE

Reposition the circles, overlapping them slightly so that all the raw edges are concealed. Pin down, then transfer the runner to the ironing board. Press down the circles with a hot iron.

## **12** EMBROIDERING THE EDGES

Thread the machine with bright fuchsia sewing thread and set the controls to a blanket or zigzag stitch. Carefully and slowly stitch around the circumference of each circle.

## **13** ADDING THE FINISHING TOUCH

Arrange the three now-pink doilies on the runner, pin them in place and stitch down by hand.

# PYJAMA TROUSERS

*These relaxed pull-on trousers are just perfect for those lazy days at home. The deep contrast cuffs can be rolled up, giving plenty of growing space.*

**YOU WILL NEED**

- 135 x 70cm Liberty Tana Lawn in print of your choice for main fabric (we used All Kinds of Families in colourway A for the boy's trousers and Nina Taylor in colourway C for the girl's trousers)
- 135 x 50cm Liberty Tana Lawn in print of your choice for the contrasting cuffs (we used Betsy Ann in colourway B for the boy's trousers and Mitsi Valeria in colourway B for the girl's trousers)
- 15mm wide elastic
- matching sewing thread
- large safety pin
- sewing machine
- sewing kit

**TEMPLATES**

Select the relevant size from the pattern templates on page 154. Enlarge the trouser leg, cuff and waistband pattern piece outlines onto dressmaker's squared paper (see page 9 for how to do this). Check the size before cutting out the fabric and make any necessary adjustments.

**CUTTING OUT**

*from Liberty Tana Lawn main print*
two legs, one reversed
(mark the back of each leg with a safety pin)

*from Liberty Tana Lawn contrast print*
two cuffs
one waistband

**FINISHED SIZES**

| To fit ages | 3–4 | 5–6 | 7–8 | years |
|---|---|---|---|---|
| To fit waist | 40 | 44 | 48 | cm |

N<small>INA</small> T<small>AYLOR</small> *is a simple design of hand-painted sandalwood leaves inspired by the fragrance 'Avignon' by Comme des Garçons.*

## ❶ ADDING THE CUFF

Press back a 1cm turning along the bottom edge of each cuff. With right sides facing, pin and tack the top edges of the cuffs to the bottom edges of the trouser legs. Machine stitch, with a 1cm seam, then press the seam allowance to one side, so that it lies over the cuff.

## ❷ JOINING THE INSIDE LEG SEAMS

With right sides facing, fold the trouser legs in half lengthways. Pin the leg seams together, carefully matching up the points where the cuff seam meets up. Tack, and then machine stitch 1cm from the edge.

## ❸ NEATENING THE SEAMS

Press open the seam allowance along the cuff, using the tip of the iron. Trim the rest of the seam allowance back to 6mm and finish off with a zigzag or overlocking stitch.

## ❹ TURNING UP THE CUFF

Fold the cuff in half and pin the neatened edge to the trouser leg, so that it lies just above the seam line. Tack in place, then turn the legs right side out and machine stitch 3mm down from the top of the cuff. Press lightly.

## ❺ SEWING THE LEGS TOGETHER

With the right sides facing, pin the two trouser legs together at the point where the two inside leg seams meet. Pin the seams together at front and back, then machine stitch with a 1cm seam. Trim the allowance back to 6mm and neaten with a zigzag or overlocking stitch.

## ❻ ADDING THE WAISTBAND

Press back a 2cm turning at both ends of the waistband and check that it fits snugly around the pyjama waist. Press back 1cm along the top edge. With right sides facing and raw edges matching, pin one end of the waistband to the front of the waistline. Pin and tack it in place all the way round, then machine stitch with a 1cm seam.

❼ Turn the folded edge over to the back so that it encloses the raw edges. Pin and tack in place, overlapping the seam line by 3mm. Machine stitch around the waistband, just inside the seam.

## ❽ THREADING THE ELASTIC

Trim one end of the elastic to a sharp point and fasten on a strong safety pin. Mark the final waist measurement on the elastic. Thread the safety pin through the gap at the front of the band, all the way round and back out the other side.

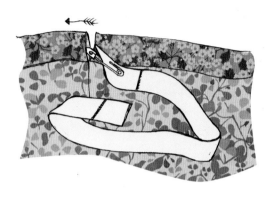

## ❾ FINISHING OFF THE WAISTBAND

Match up the end of the elastic with the mark made in step 8 and machine stitch very securely through both sides of the elastic. Trim off the ends and swivel the elastic round so that the join lies inside the waistband. Slip stitch the gap to close. Make a tiny tab of contrasting fabric and sew it to the inside back edge of the waistband so that the trousers will always be worn the right way round.

## ❿ ADDING A BOW

The girl's version has a tiny bow. Cut a 20 x 5cm strip of fabric and fold in half lengthways with right sides facing. Pin together, then machine stitch round the three sides with a 5mm seam allowance, leaving a 3cm gap in the centre of the long side. Clip the corners and turn right side out by pushing the ends through the gap with a pencil. Push out the corners and press flat. Tie into a bow and sew very securely to the waistband.

# PICNIC BAG

*This practical carry-all, with an ample amount of pockets both inside and out, provides the perfect picnic accessory for summer days spent outdoors.*

**YOU WILL NEED**

- 110 x 100cm heavyweight cream canvas or linen fabric
- 112 x 50cm Liberty Lifestyle craft fabric in print of your choice (we used Copeland in colourway E)
- 110 x 50cm plain cotton fabric in matching colour
- 3.5m of 2.5cm-wide heavy cotton webbing
- 10 x 38cm corrugated plastic, for the base
- 75 x 50cm fusible bonding web
- double-sided carpet tape
- matching sewing thread
- dressmaker's squared paper
- sharp pencil
- sewing machine
- sewing kit

**CUTTING OUT**

*from canvas or linen fabric*
side panels      two 55 x 40cm rectangles

*from plain cotton fabric*
lining      two 55 x 40cm rectangles
pocket bindings   six 25 x 8cm strips

*from Liberty Lifestyle craft fabric*
inner pocket      two 25 x 20cm rectangles

**TEMPLATE**
Copy the template on page 156, enlarging it by 200%, and cut out the outer pocket pattern piece.

## ❶ MAKING THE OUTSIDE POCKETS
The stiffened outside pockets are made by fusing together two layers of fabric. Draw round the outer pocket template six times onto the paper side of the bonding web and cut out just outside the outline.

**COPELAND** *is based on a 1965 design by Friedlande di Colbertaldo Dinzl for Liberty. It was printed at Liberty's Merton Abbey Print Works on silk in 1966.*

**2** Following the manufacturer's instructions, position the shapes, with the paper side upwards, on the wrong side of the Liberty Lifestyle craft fabric. Press them down with a hot iron and then roughly cut out. Peel off the backing papers, press the pockets onto the canvas and cut out along the pencil outlines.

### **3** BINDING THE POCKET EDGES

Press a 5mm turning along one long edge of each binding strip. With right sides facing, pin and tack the raw edges of the strips centrally to the front of the pockets, in line with the top edge. Machine in place, 15mm from the edge of the binding. Turn the folded edge to the wrong side and slip stitch down.

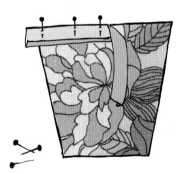

### **4** PREPARING THE BAG SIDES

Both sides of the bag are made in the same way. Draw a 5cm square at the bottom corners of both side panels and cut out.

### **5** MARKING THE GUIDELINES

Draw a pencil line across the panel, 9cm up from the bottom edge. Measure the centre of this line and mark two points 8cm and 9cm away from it on each side. Draw two vertical 25cm lines from these points. Mark them 5cm down from the top edge: this is where the top edge of the pockets will lie. Add two more lines, 1cm in from the outside edges.

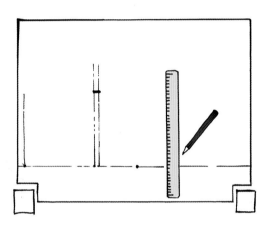

## ❻ SEWING ON THE POCKETS

Remember to change your machine needle to a strong size 90 when sewing through the canvas. Line the bottom edge of the first pocket up with the centre section of the pencil line, then pin and tack it in place. Sew down with a wide zigzag stitch, reinforcing both ends of the line with a few reverse stitches. Join the side edges along the vertical lines in the same way. The pocket will now project out from the bag. Add one more pocket on each side, following the other pencil lines. Repeat for the second panel.

## ❽ CONCEALING THE RAW EDGES

Cut two 55cm lengths of webbing. Pin and tack one to each bag panel, 8cm up from the bottom edge. Check that the ends line up at the sides of both panels and stitch down the webbing as before.

## ❾ JOINING THE PANELS

Place the two panels together with right sides facing. Pin and tack the side and bottom edges, carefully matching the points where the pockets and tape meet. Machine stitch 2cm from the edge.

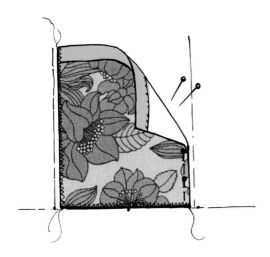

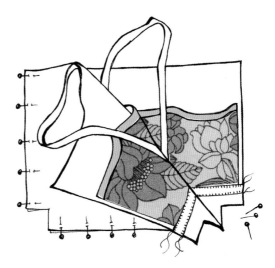

## ❼ ADDING THE HANDLES

Cut two 1m lengths of webbing. Pin the ends of one to each panel between the top of the pencil lines and the bottom edge. Tack in place then sew down with matching thread, using a machine blanket stitch or zigzag stitch.

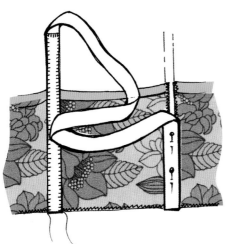

127

## ⑩ STITCHING THE CORNERS

Press the seams open from the wrong side, using the tip of the iron so you don't crush the pockets. Re-fold the open corners at an angle so the side and bottom seams meet in the middle. Pin and tack together, then machine stitch taking a 15mm seam allowance.

## ⑪ REINFORCING THE OPENING AND BASE

Press back a 1.5cm turning around the top edge of the bag and sew it down with three rounds of wide zigzag stitch. Press under another 2cm turning. Place the plastic rectangle inside the bag to check it fits snugly within the base. Trim if necessary, then secure in place with double-sided carpet tape.

## ⑫ MAKING THE INNER POCKET

Sew a double 8mm hem along the top edge of one inner pocket piece. With right sides facing, pin and tack both pieces together, matching the side and bottom edges. Machine stitch 10mm from the edge, then trim back the seam allowance to 6mm and neaten with a zigzag or overlock stitch. Turn the pocket right side out and press.

## ⑬ ADDING THE LINING

Join the two lining pieces as for the main bag, sewing the side and bottom seams first, then the corners. Press the seams open, but keep it wrong side out. Slip the lining inside the bag, matching the side seams, then pin the top edge around the opening in line with the bottom of the hem. Pin the inner pocket centrally to one side of the bag, 1cm down from the top of the lining, and tack through all the layers.

⑭ Fold and tack the top hem of the bag over once again to enclose the raw edges of the lining and stitch it down 3mm from the folded edge. Work a final round of stitches 3mm down from the top edge.

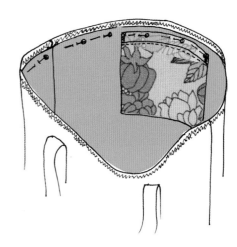

# PET BED

*Every dog or cat lover's home houses a pet bed, but often they are tricky to find in attractive fabrics. Making your own from robust Liberty print needlecord solves this decor dilemma.*

**YOU WILL NEED**

- 140 x 170cm Liberty Kingly Cord in print of your choice (we used Jack and Charlie in colourway A)
- 80 x 60cm plain furnishing fabric
- 750g safety standard polyester toy filling
- matching sewing thread
- sewing machine
- dressmaker's squared paper
- sewing kit

**TEMPLATE**
Copy the template on page 156, enlarging it by 200%, and cut out the side panel pattern piece.

**CUTTING OUT**

### from Liberty Kingly Cord
Make sure that the top edges of the front panel, back panel and sides all line up on the same part of the pattern repeat.

| | |
|---|---|
| front panels | two 75 x 25cm rectangles |
| back panels | two 75 x 25cm rectangles |
| side panels | four 50 x 25cm rectangles |
| inside base | one 75 x 50cm rectangle |

### from plain furnishing fabric
| | |
|---|---|
| outside base | one 75 x 50cm rectangle |

Prepare the inner and outer bases by marking a 15mm square at each corner.

**NOTE**
The seam allowance is 1.5cm throughout.

**JACK AND CHARLIE** *is a conversational pear print inspired by a furnishing design in the Liberty archive originally created in the early 1990s by the Jack Prince Studio.*

## ❶ SHAPING THE FRONT PANELS

Draw up the full-size template onto dressmaker's squared paper. Fold a front panel piece in half crossways and pin the template through both layers, with the left edge lying over the fold. Cut along the curved edge. Cut out the other panel in the same way.

## ❷ JOINING THE TOP PIECES

With right sides facing, pin the ends of two side panels to a back panel. Pin a front panel to the other two ends. Machine stitch, from the top corner downwards, leaving the bottom 1.5cm unstitched and reinforcing both ends of each seam with a few reverse stitches. Press the seams open. Join the other two side panels to the other back panel and the other front panel in the same way for the inside of the bed.

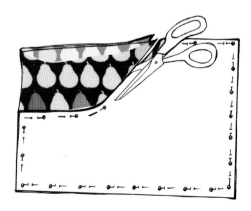

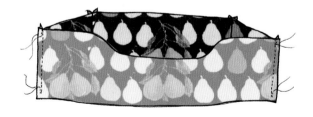

### ❸ ADDING THE BASE

With right sides facing, pin and tack the bottom edge of the outside top to the front, back and sides of the plain outside base. The pressed back seam allowances should line up with the edges of the corner squares.

❹ With the top uppermost, machine stitch together with a 1.5cm seam, turning the fabric through 90 degrees at each corner. Reinforce the stitching at each corner. Press the seam open.

❺ Make up the outer bed in the same way, but leave a 40cm opening in the centre of the back seam. Press back the seam allowance on each side of this opening.

### ❻ JOINING THE INSIDE AND OUTSIDE

With right sides facing, pin the two beds together, lining up the corner seams. Pin, tack and machine stitch all the way around the upper edge. Clip into the seam allowance along the curves (see page 13 for how to do this), then turn the whole thing right side out through the opening at the back.

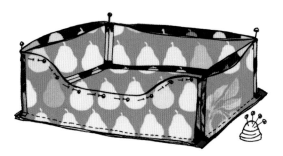

### ❼ STUFFING THE BED

Using a double length of sewing thread, and small running stitches, sew the two layers together along the four corner seams.

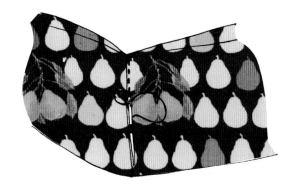

❽ Reaching right inside the cover, stuff the front section with toy filling, distributing it evenly. Close the section by pinning the inside and outside together along the seam line. Hand stitch along this line as for the sides. Fill the side and back sections in the same way, then stuff the base. Sew the two sides of the opening securely together to complete.

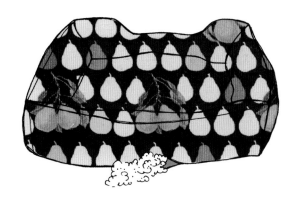

# SEWING MACHINE COVER AND BAG

*Liven up your sewing machine when it's not in use by making this slip-on dust cover. The additional drawstring bag stores the machine's foot pedal or other sewing effects.*

### for the sewing machine cover
- 120 x 115cm heavy calico fabric
- 110 x 30cm Liberty Tana Lawn in print of your choice for the main print (we used Manuela in colourway E)
- 135 x 20cm Liberty Tana Lawn in print of your choice for the contrasting print (we used Marco in colourway A)
- 30 x 20cm fusible bonding web
- sharp pencil
- air-erasable pen or chalk pencil
- matching and contrasting sewing threads
- sewing machine
- sewing kit

### for the drawstring bag
- 40 x 65cm Liberty Tana Lawn in print of your choice for the main print (we used Manuela in colourway E)
- 45 x 75cm Liberty Tana Lawn in print of your choice for the contrasting print (we used Marco in colourway A)
- 2m of 12mm-wide ribbon
- four 2cm-diameter wooden beads
- large safety pin

### SIZING NOTE
The pattern is designed to fit most standard domestic sewing machines. Copy and enlarge the side panel template from page 155 and check the size against your machine, adjusting the width and height if necessary. You may then need to alter the length of the main cover accordingly.

### TEMPLATES
Copy the templates on page 155, copying the tie end template at 100% and enlarging all the other templates by 200%. Cut out the side panel, pocket, sewing machine motif and tie end pattern pieces.

#### CUTTING OUT

#### FOR THE SEWING MACHINE COVER

##### from calico fabric
| | |
|---|---|
| main cover | one 45 x 68cm rectangle |
| lining | one 45 x 70cm rectangle |
| two side panels | |
| two pockets | |

##### from Liberty Tana Lawn main print
two side panels

##### from Liberty Tana Lawn contrasting print
| | |
|---|---|
| cover edging | two 45 x 3cm strips |
| pocket edging | two 25 x 8cm strips |

#### FOR THE DRAWSTRING BAG

##### from Liberty Tana Lawn main print
| | |
|---|---|
| main bag | one 32 x 58cm rectangle |

##### from Liberty Tana Lawn contrasting print
| | |
|---|---|
| lining | one 32 x 68cm rectangle |
| four tie ends, cut on the fold | |

## *making the sewing machine cover*

### ❶ CUTTING OUT THE APPLIQUÉ SHAPES

Trace the reversed sewing machine, handle and cotton reel onto the paper side of the fusible bonding web with a sharp pencil and roughly cut out the three shapes. Following the manufacturer's instructions, iron the sewing machine shape onto the back of the main print fabric, and the handle and reel onto the contrasting print fabric.

❷ Cut neatly around each outline and peel off the backing papers. Position the sewing machine shape on the main calico cover piece, 7cm up from the bottom edge. Press in place, then add the handle and cotton reel.

### ❸ STITCHING AROUND THE SHAPES

Using an air-erasable pen or chalk pencil, draw in the swirling line of thread. Using a narrow satin or blanket stitch, machine stitch around the edge of the sewing machine shape using a thread to match the fabric. Change to a contrasting sewing thread, then stitch around the handle, the cotton reel and along the thread line.

### ❹ EDGING THE MAIN CALICO COVER PIECE

With right sides facing, pin an edging strip to each short edge of the main calico cover. Tack in place, then machine stitch 1cm from the edge. Press the seam allowance over the Tana Lawn.

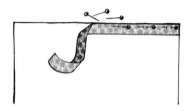

### ❺ EDGING THE POCKETS

Fold the pocket edging in half lengthways with the right side facing outwards. Pin the folded strip centrally to the wrong side of the pocket, along the top edge, matching the raw edges. Machine stitch, leaving a seam allowance of 1cm, then turn the edging over to the right side and press. Trim the ends in line with the side edges of the pocket.

### ❻ JOINING ON THE POCKETS

Fold the side panel in half lengthways and mark the centre top. Pin and tack the completed pocket to the panel, matching the side and bottom edges.

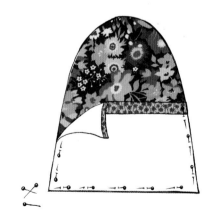

## ❼ MAKING UP THE MAIN COVER

Fold the cover in half crossways and mark the centre of each side edge. With right sides facing, pin on one of the side panels, matching up the centre points and the corners. Tack the two together close to the edge and machine stitch, leaving a 6mm seam allowance. Add the second side panel in the same way. Turn right side out and press lightly.

## ❽ ASSEMBLING THE LINING

Make up the calico lining in the same way, but leave a 15cm gap along the edge of one side panel. Press back the seam allowance on both sides of the opening.

## ❾ SEWING THE LINING TO THE COVER

With right sides facing, slip the lining inside the main cover. Matching up the four seams, pin the two bottom edges together. Tack and machine stitch 1cm from the edge. Turn right side out through the opening, then slip stitch the gap to close. Now push the lining back inside the cover. Press the bottom edge so that 1cm of the lining projects beyond the seam line. Machine stitch along the seam to stabilise the hem.

## *making the drawstring bag*

## ❶ MAKING UP THE MAIN BAG

Place the two rectangles together with right sides facing. Pin and tack the side and bottom edges, then machine stitch with a 1cm seam. Now clip a small triangle from each bottom corner and press the seam allowances inwards. Turn the bag right side out.

## ❷ PREPARING THE DRAWSTRING CHANNEL

With the wrong side of the fabric facing upwards, press back a 2cm turning along the top edge of each lining piece, then fold back and press a second turning, this time 3cm wide. Unfold both creases.

### ❸ MAKING UP THE LINING

Pin and tack the two pieces together with right sides facing, then machine stitch the side and bottom edges with a 1cm seam. Leave a 2cm gap in each side seam, centrally positioned between the two fold lines. This will be the opening for the ribbons.

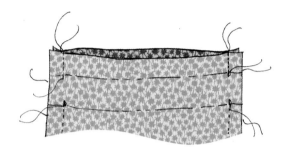

❹ Clip a small triangle from the bottom corners, then press the seam allowance inwards as for the main bag. Hand stitch down the seam allowance on each side of the opening. Re-fold and re-press the turnings.

### ❺ JOINING THE BAG AND LINING

With the bag right side out and the lining wrong side out, slip the lining inside the bag and push it right down into the bottom corners. Fold the turning over the top edge of the main bag, matching up the side seams. Pin and tack it down. Using matching thread, machine stitch twice around the turning, 5mm from the top edge and 5mm from the bottom edge.

### ❻ THREADING THROUGH THE TIES

Cut the ribbon in half. Fix a safety pin to one end of the first ribbon and feed it through one of the openings. Push it all the way round the channel and back out. Thread the second ribbon through the other opening in the same way.

### ❼ ADDING THE BEADS

Trim the ends of the ribbon into narrow points and thread a bead onto each one. Push the beads halfway up the ribbons and cut off the points.

### ❽ MAKING UP THE TIE ENDS

Press the tie ends in half lengthways with right sides facing. Turn back and press both top edges along the fold line. Tack the side edges and machine stitch with a 6mm seam. Clip the corners and turn right side out, using a pencil to ease out the corners.

❾ Push the ends of the ribbons into the tie ends. Tack them in place, then machine stitch close to the top edge. Slide the beads back down the ribbons: the ties ends will gather slightly.

# UPHOLSTERED FOOTSTOOL

*The flat, smooth surface of a footstool is the perfect canvas for showcasing a favourite print. Why not reclaim an old stool and update the woodwork with a bright shade of paint.*

**YOU WILL NEED**

- Liberty Linen Union in print of your choice (we used Sydenham Hall in colourway A), see right to calculate the amount of fabric needed
- polyester wadding, 2cm smaller all round than the fabric
- block of upholstery foam cut to size, if needed
- matching sewing thread
- double-sided carpet tape
- upholsterer's nails
- small hammer
- air-erasable pen or chalk pencil
- long ruler
- sewing machine
- sewing kit
- medium grain sandpaper
- white spirit
- spray primer and paint
  or
- paintbrush, wood primer and wood paint
- clear varnish

**MEASURING UP**

Measure the width (A), depth (B) and height (C) of the foam block, and the height of the footstool base (D) and use these figures to calculate the size of the wadding and fabric.

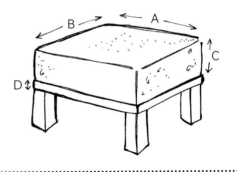

**CUTTING OUT**

*from polyester wadding*
one rectangle   width = A + 2C
                depth = B + 2C
                cut one square 2cm less than
                than C from each corner

*from Liberty Linen Union*
one rectangle   width = A + 2C + 2D + 4cm
                depth = B + 2C + 2D + 4cm

## ❶ RENOVATING THE FOOTSTOOL BASE

Remove the existing fabric and tacks. If the original foam is still in good condition, leave it in place and replace the fabric cover to protect it from any stray paint. Rub down the frame and legs with medium-grain sandpaper.

❷ Remove any dust and dirt with white spirit and apply the appropriate primer. Finish with two coats of wood paint or four light coats of spray paint, taking care to cover every bit of wood. For a more protected finish, paint with clear varnish. Leave to dry. If you are using new foam, fix it to the top of the stool with double-sided carpet tape.

❸ Lay the wadding over the foam and trim the bottom edges in line with the top of the stool. This extra layer will give a smooth look to the cover.

## ❹ MARKING THE GUIDELINES ON THE FABRIC

Lay the fabric out with the right side facing downwards and, using an air-erasable pen or chalk pencil and a long ruler, mark the guidelines. First, draw a line 2cm in from each side edge, then four lines parallel to these, which lie the same as the height of the foam (measurement 'C') further in.

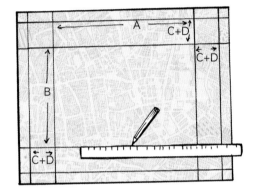

## ❺ JOINING THE CORNERS

Press back and then unfold the 2cm turning around the outside edge. Fold the fabric. With right sides facing, fold the cover so that the right-hand edge lies along the bottom edge. Pin the front and back together, matching up the guidelines. Join the other corners in the same way, then slip the cover over the stool.

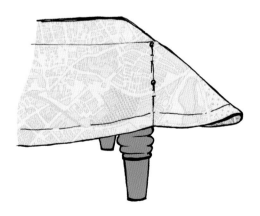

## ❻ MAKING UP THE COVER

Adjust the pins if necessary to get a perfect fit, then tack the seams in line with the pins. Machine stitch from the outside edge inwards, to within 6mm of the point where the guidelines meet. Adjust the angle so the final few stitches slope slightly to the left and continue to the end. This will give a neatly rounded look to the corners.

## ❼ PRESSING THE SEAMS AND HEMMING

Trim away the excess fabric at the corners, leaving a 1cm seam allowance and tapering it to 4mm at the top. Press the four seams open. Turn up and re-press the bottom hem, then tack it down. If you wish, you can tack a round of contrasting braid over the hem as a background for the nails.

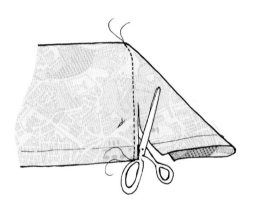

## ❽ MARKING THE NAIL POSITIONS

Make a series of pencil or chalk marks around the top edge of the footstool so the nails will be regularly spaced. Start by marking the midpoint of each side, then a point 1cm in from each corner. Divide the rest of the length at 3–4cm intervals.

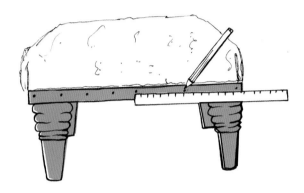

## ❾ FIXING DOWN THE COVER

Starting at one midpoint, gently pull the fabric down until the edge is level with the bottom edge of the footstool top. Insert an upholsterer's nail through the hem so the rim of the nail touches the edge of the fabric. Hammer it in, at right angles to the stool. Repeat on the opposite side, then the other two sides. Fix in the corner nails, then add the rest, working from the centre outwards. Always repeat on one side what you do on the other to maintain the fabric at an even tension across the top of the footstool.

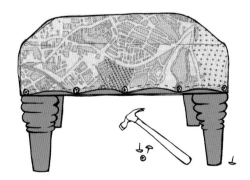

# STRIPED THROW

─────── ● ───────

*The beauty of this quilt is its random, spontaneous juxtaposition of fabrics, made easy by the fact that so many Liberty Tana Lawn prints work effortlessly together.*

**YOU WILL NEED**

- 1m of 135cm wide Liberty Tana Lawn in classic print of your choice for the main print (we used Wiltshire in colourway R)
- 50cm of 135cm wide Liberty Tana Lawn in each of five further prints (we used Felix and Isabelle in colourway B; Kayoko in colourway D; Mabelle in colourway C; Mark Gosling in colourway C; Small Susanna in colourway D)
- 155cm square cotton quilt wadding
- matching sewing thread
- quilting thread
- sewing machine
- sewing kit
- one or two thimbles
- quilter's safety pins

**FINISHED SIZE**
The finished throw measures approximately 146cm square.

**CUTTING OUT**

*from Liberty Tana Lawn main print*
Join two pieces to reach the required length for the side borders and the binding.

| | |
|---|---|
| top border | one 130 x 10cm strip |
| bottom border | one 130 x 10cm strip |
| side borders | two 10 x 146cm strips |
| binding | four 150 x 5cm strips |

## ❶ MAKING THE CENTRE PANEL

The centre panel is made up of randomly arranged stripes, each one a narrow strip of Tana Lawn between 5cm and 8cm wide. The quickest way to prepare these is to make a small snip into the selvedge, tear across the full width of the fabric and press well to flatten out the edges. Pin two strips together lengthways with right sides facing and machine stitch, taking a 1cm seam allowance.

**❷** Press the seam to one side. Continue adding more strips, alternating the fabrics, until the panel is 130cm deep. Line up all the strips on the left-hand side and press all the seam allowances in the same direction. Trim the right edge so that it is perfectly straight. Measure a point 130cm along the top and bottom edges and rule a line between them. Cut along this line to give you a square.

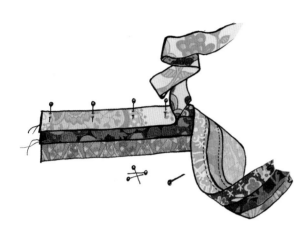

### ❸ ADDING THE BORDERS

Sew the top and bottom borders to the finished centre panel with a 1cm seam and press the seams outwards. Add the two side borders, again pressing the seams outwards, and trim the ends as necessary.

### ❹ MAKING THE BACKING

Sew the backing together in the same way, using 10–20cm wide strips of the remaining fabric to make a rectangle 160cm long by 130cm wide. Press the seams open. Make two 17 x 160cm strips and sew one to each side edge with a 1cm seam, for a 160cm-square backing.

### ❺ ASSEMBLING THE LAYERS

Spread out the backing, with the right side facing downwards, and place the wadding centrally on top. Lay the front of the quilt centrally over the wadding, with the right side facing upwards. Smooth out the sandwiched layers and, working across from one edge, safety pin them together at 10cm intervals.

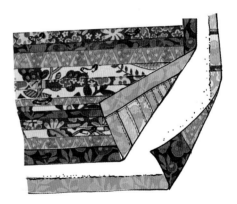

### ❻ HAND QUILTING THE SEAMS

The ridged look is created by quilting the seams 'in the ditch' or directly on top of the join between the strips. Sew a line of 5mm running stitches along each seam with quilting thread, preferably using one or two thimbles to protect your fingers.

**7** When the quilting is complete, tack around the outside edge of the quilt front to hold the three layers together. Cut off the surplus wadding and backing fabric.

## **8** BINDING THE TOP AND BOTTOM EDGES

Press under a 1cm turning along one long edge of each binding strip. With right sides facing pin the first strip centrally to the top edge of the quilt, matching the raw edges and leaving an overlap at each end.

**9** Machine stitch 1cm from the edge, then turn the binding to the back to enclose the raw edges. Pin down the folded edge, trim the ends in line with the sides of the quilt and slip stitch the fold to the quilt. Bind the bottom edge in the same way.

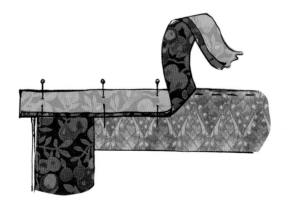

## **10** BINDING THE SIDE EDGES

Press under a 1cm turning at the end of both remaining binding strips. Line the folded end up with the neatened edge of the quilt and pin the strip to the quilt as for the top and bottom edges. Trim the other end so that it is 1cm longer than the quilt and fold under this overlap.

**11** Sew the strip in place and turn the folded edge over to the wrong side. Slip stitch the fold to the quilt.

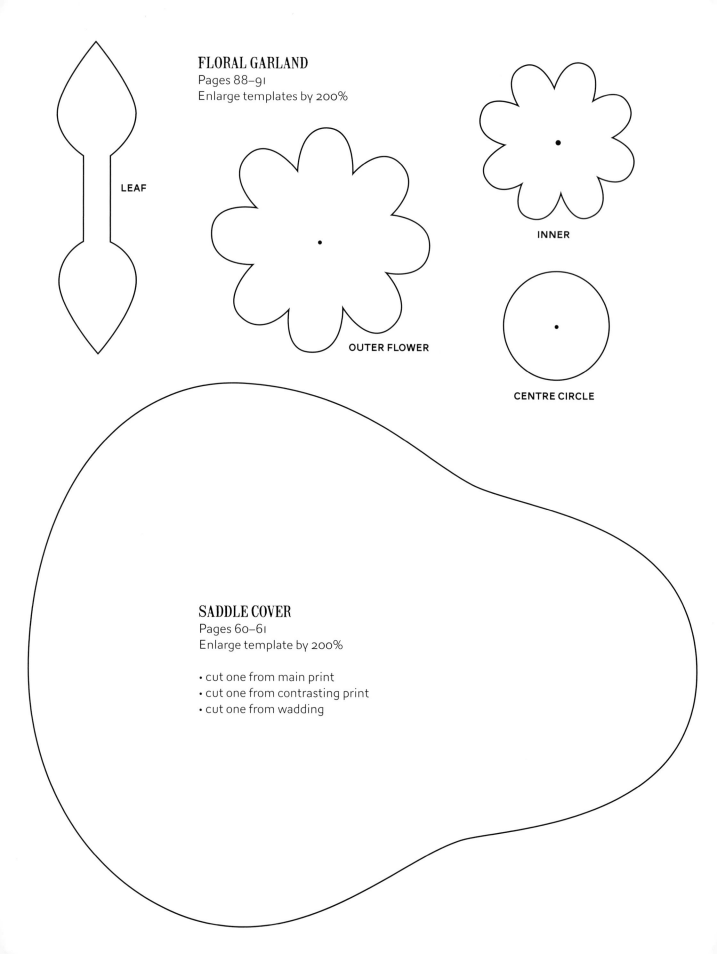

**LEAF**

# FLORAL GARLAND
Pages 88–91
Enlarge templates by 200%

**OUTER FLOWER**

**INNER**

**CENTRE CIRCLE**

# SADDLE COVER
Pages 60–61
Enlarge template by 200%

• cut one from main print
• cut one from contrasting print
• cut one from wadding

# CAFETIERE COVER

Pages 62–65
Enlarge templates by 200%

**TAB**
cut one from paper

velcro

**COVER**
• cut one from paper

# CLOUD CUSHIONS AND CLOUD MOBILE

Pages 18–23
Enlarge template at 250% for small cloud
cushion, 325% for medium cloud cushion
and 400% for large cloud cushion
Enlarge template at 130% for small cloud
mobile and 160% for large cloud mobile

• cut two (one reversed)

opening

# 'LIBBY' DOLL
Pages 80–87
Enlarge templates by 200%

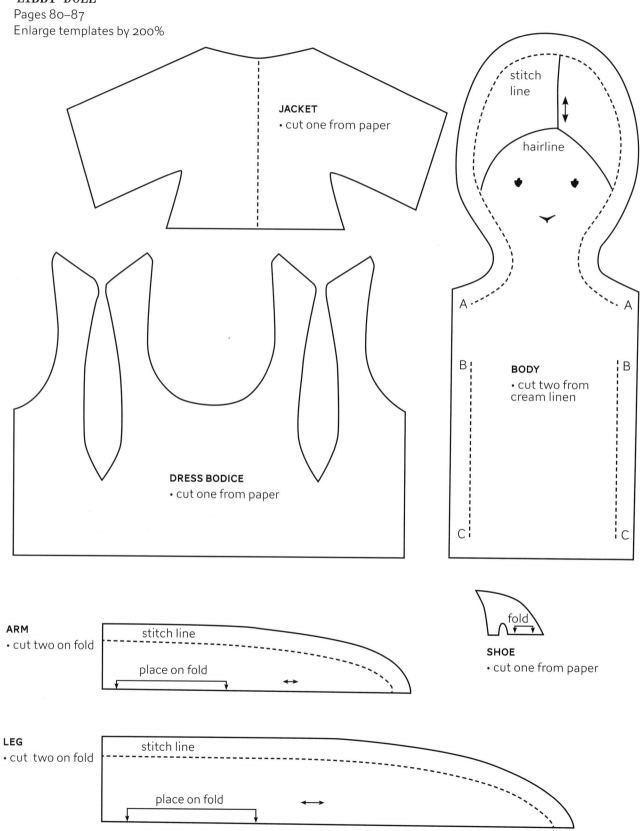

**JACKET**
• cut one from paper

stitch line

hairline

**DRESS BODICE**
• cut one from paper

A — A

B — B

**BODY**
• cut two from cream linen

C — C

**SHOE**
• cut one from paper

fold

**ARM**
• cut two on fold

stitch line

place on fold

**LEG**
• cut two on fold

stitch line

place on fold

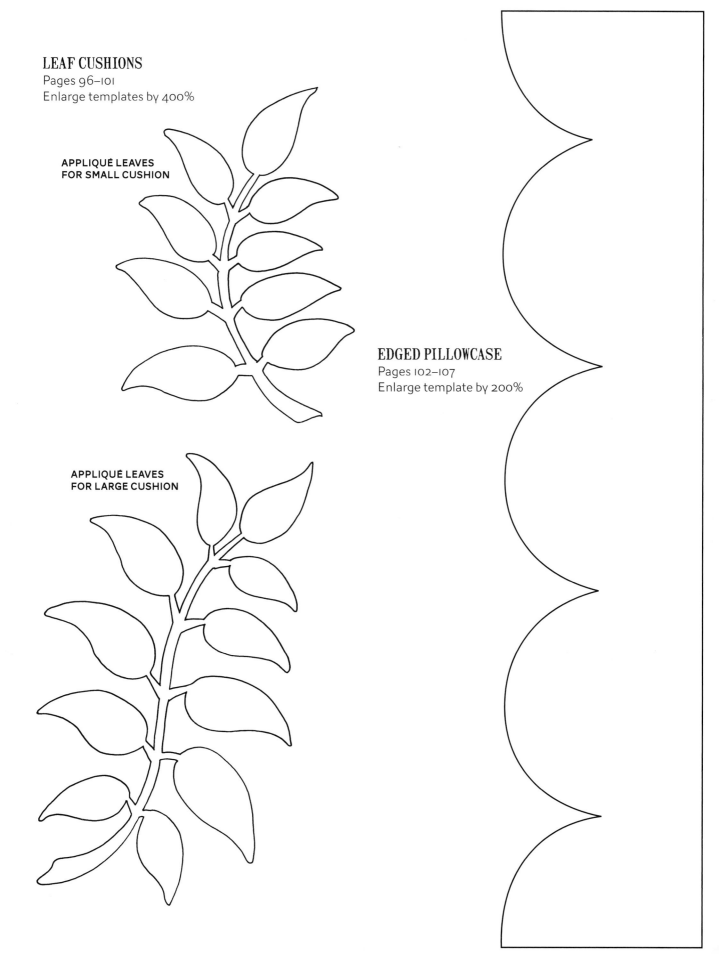

# LEAF CUSHIONS
Pages 96–101
Enlarge templates by 400%

**APPLIQUÉ LEAVES
FOR SMALL CUSHION**

## EDGED PILLOWCASE
Pages 102–107
Enlarge template by 200%

**APPLIQUÉ LEAVES
FOR LARGE CUSHION**

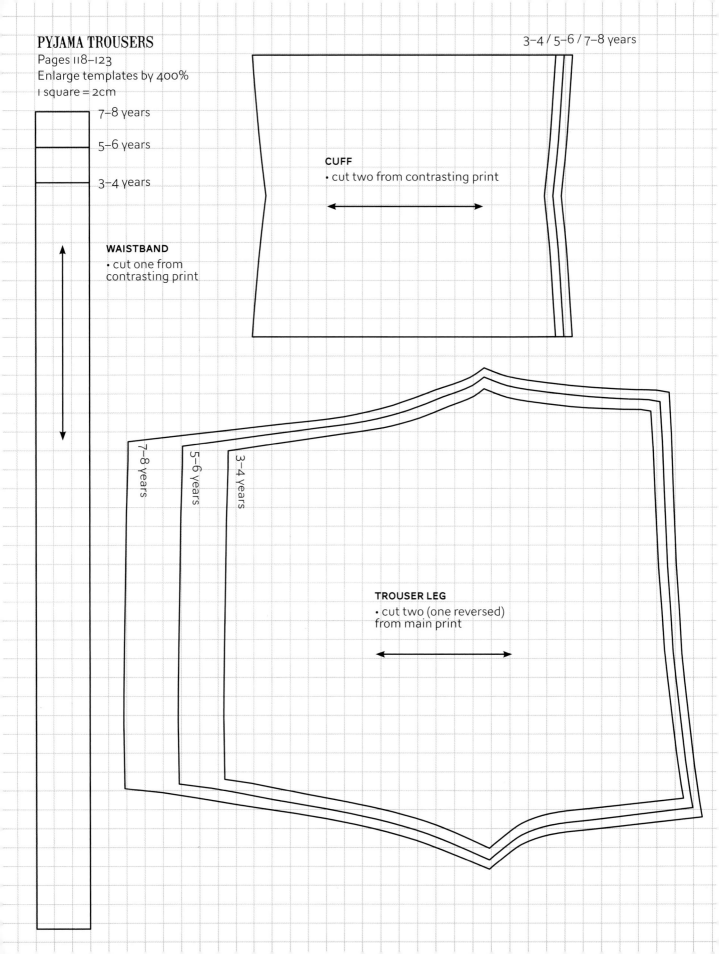

# PYJAMA TROUSERS

Pages 118–123

Enlarge templates by 400%

1 square = 2cm

3–4 / 5–6 / 7–8 years

7–8 years

5–6 years

3–4 years

**WAISTBAND**
• cut one from
contrasting print

**CUFF**
• cut two from contrasting print

7–8 years

5–6 years

3–4 years

**TROUSER LEG**
• cut two (one reversed)
from main print

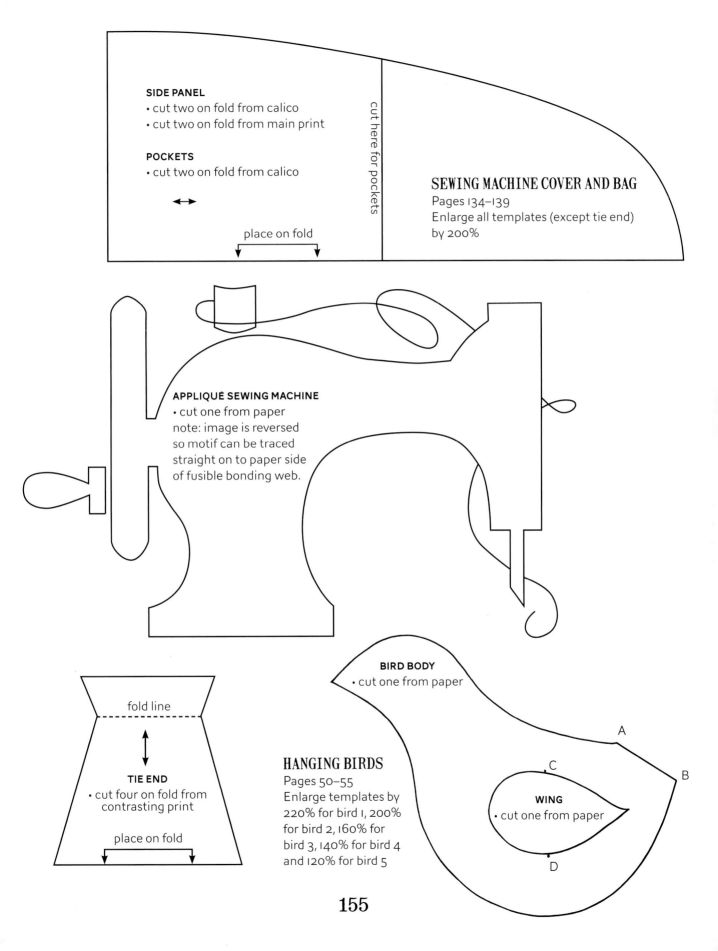

**SIDE PANEL**
• cut two on fold from calico
• cut two on fold from main print

**POCKETS**
• cut two on fold from calico

place on fold

cut here for pockets

# SEWING MACHINE COVER AND BAG
Pages 134–139
Enlarge all templates (except tie end)
by 200%

**APPLIQUÉ SEWING MACHINE**
• cut one from paper
note: image is reversed
so motif can be traced
straight on to paper side
of fusible bonding web.

fold line

**TIE END**
• cut four on fold from
contrasting print

place on fold

# HANGING BIRDS
Pages 50–55
Enlarge templates by
220% for bird 1, 200%
for bird 2, 160% for
bird 3, 140% for bird 4
and 120% for bird 5

**BIRD BODY**
• cut one from paper

A

C

B

**WING**
• cut one from paper

D

**OUTER POCKET**
• cut one from paper

## PICNIC BAG
Pages 124–129
Enlarge template by 200%

## PET BED
Pages 130–133
Enlarge template by 200%

**FRONT PANEL**
• cut two on fold from main print

place on fold

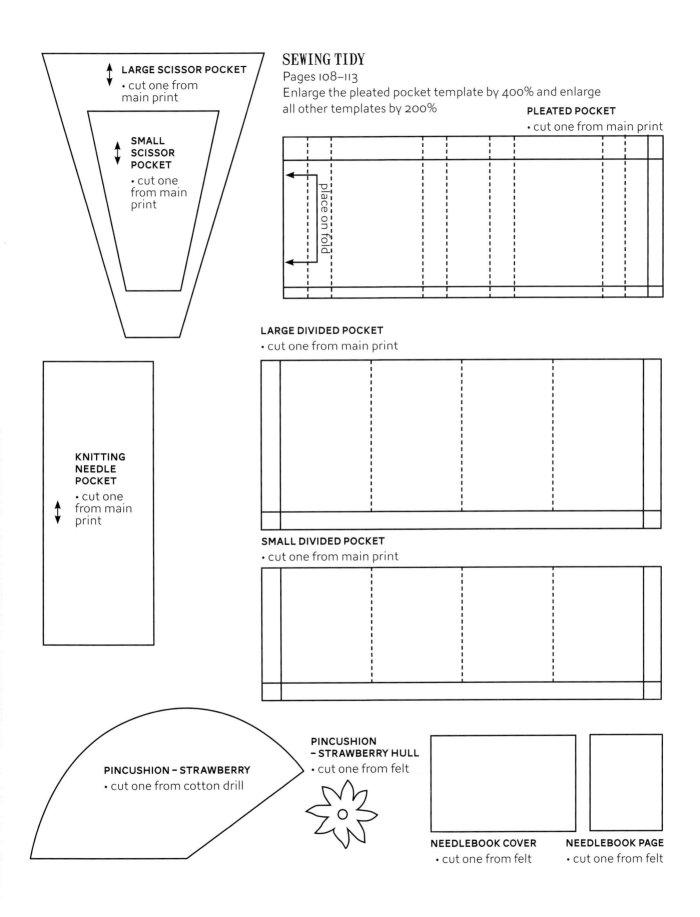

**LARGE SCISSOR POCKET**
• cut one from main print

**SMALL SCISSOR POCKET**
• cut one from main print

# SEWING TIDY

Pages 108–113
Enlarge the pleated pocket template by 400% and enlarge all other templates by 200%

**PLEATED POCKET**
• cut one from main print

place on fold

**KNITTING NEEDLE POCKET**
• cut one from main print

**LARGE DIVIDED POCKET**
• cut one from main print

**SMALL DIVIDED POCKET**
• cut one from main print

**PINCUSHION – STRAWBERRY**
• cut one from cotton drill

**PINCUSHION – STRAWBERRY HULL**
• cut one from felt

**NEEDLEBOOK COVER**
• cut one from felt

**NEEDLEBOOK PAGE**
• cut one from felt

## LIFESTYLE CRAFT FABRIC

**BELL** is based on a 1963 Liberty design. It was printed at Liberty's Merton Abbey Print Works on varuna wool.

**CATHERINE** is based on a 1969 design. It was printed at Liberty's Merton Abbey Print Works on varuna wool in 1971.

**COPELAND** is based on a 1965 design by Friedlande di Colbertaldo Dinzl for Liberty. It was printed at Liberty's Merton Abbey Print Works on silk in 1966.

**CRANSTON** is based on an early 1900s artwork found in the Liberty archive.

**DANCE** is based on a 1991 design by the Jack Prince Studio. It was used in the spring/ summer collection of 1993.

**GARNETT** is based on several 1930s Liberty designs. It was printed at Liberty's Merton Abbey Print Works on wool in 1971.

**HERBERT** is based on a Liberty design from the early 1900s, when Liberty was renowned for its iconic Art Nouveau designs.

**LEONARD** was designed by Sholto Drumlanrig, who put together the Liberty Lifestyle craft fabric collection.

**LOWKE** is based on a Liberty furnishing cretonne from the late 1890s.

**MACKINTOSH** is inspired by the early 1900s Glasgow School artists and was designed by Sholto Drumlanrig.

**NEWBURY** is based on a 1965 design by Agnes Roberts for Liberty. It was printed at Liberty's Merton Abbey Print Works on cotton in 1966.

**RENNIE** is based on a Liberty furnishing linen from the early 1900s.

**WOOLF** is based on a 1977 design by Allan Thomas for Liberty. It was used in the spring/ summer collection of 1979.

## KINGLY CORD

**JACK AND CHARLIE** is a conversational pear print inspired by a furnishing design in the Liberty archive, originally created in the early 1990s by the Jack Prince Studio.

## MADAURI COTTON

**INDIRA** is based on a printed gauze design from the late nineteenth century found in the Liberty archive.

**PRIYA** is based on a bold one-colour pattern that was designed especially for the Liberty spring/summer collection of 2007.

**TEHZEEB** is based on an indigo printed cotton sample from an early 1900s Liberty pattern book.

**ZAI** is based on a 1995 design by Michael Fieldsend for Liberty, which was used in the spring/summer collection of 1998.

## FURNISHING COLLECTION

**FELIX RAISON** was inspired by a Liberty dress fabric design that was based on an 1850s paisley shawl drawing found in the Liberty archive.

**HEBE** is a one-colour version of Liberty's famous peacock feather pattern. This design has been in the range since the 1890s and is one of the key prints associated with Liberty.

**SEPTEMBER ROSLYND** is a hand-drawn Art Nouveau graphic design from a dress fabric for the autumn/winter collection of 2009.

**SYDENHAM HALL** is based on old maps of Crystal Palace, designed for a spring/summer 2004 dress fabric.

## TANA LAWN

**ALL KINDS OF FAMILIES** is taken from the fingerprints of all the designers in the Liberty Design Studio. The pattern was hand painted and then coloured to create an all-over tonal texture.

**ARANOV** is a graphic hand-drawn lady-and-bird design inspired by the romance of the Secession movement.

**BETSY ANN** is a miniature version of the famous Liberty classic print 'Betsy' which originated in 1933.

**FARHAD** was inspired by Art Nouveau repeats and mazes of stately gardens in Vienna. The design captures motifs from both art and nature.

**FELIX AND ISABELLE** was based on a drawing of a paisley shawl from the 1850s found in the Liberty archive.

**GLENJADE** was created from a 1930s Liberty cotton design. The designer is unknown but the print has been in the Classic Tana collection since 1979.

**HUGO GRENVILLE** is named after the very established botanical painter. This design is based upon his paintings from the Tresco Abbey Garden.

**JOLIE ROSE** was created from the drawings and paintings of five-year-olds at a Parisian primary school. The repeat was inspired by the Breton stripe.

**KATIE AND MILLIE** is a small floral trail inspired by a design from the Liberty archive originally created in the 1920s.

**KAYOKO** is an archival floral design from the Liberty Art Fabrics spring/summer collection of 2011.

**LODDEN** is an original William Morris design, first produced by Morris & Co in 1884.

**MABELLE** is inspired by Indian chintz designs of the seventeenth and eighteenth centuries. It was created by the Liberty Design studio especially for the Classic Tana collection in 2007.

**MANUELA** was inspired by a scarf design from the Liberty archive created in the 1970s. During this period many of Liberty's patterns were based on Liberty's 1930s floral designs.

**MARC GOSLING** is a geometric leaf design inspired by a rare type of Heliconia.

**MARCO** was a print of tiny trees that was re-traced from the original and printed on tints and deep-dyed grounds to create solid blocks of colour.

**MARINA SEAFLOWER** is hand-painted from the lush and exotic flora found in the Tresco Abbey Garden.

**MAUVERINA** is a modern Art Nouveau floral created by the Liberty Design Studio for the autumn/winter collection 2007.

**MAUVEY** is a mixture of Mallow flowers and sequins, created by Liberty's Design Studio for the spring/summer collection of 2008. It was re-scaled for the Classic Tana range in 2011.

**MAY ROSE** was hand-drawn from sunflowers to represent the annual worldwide sunflower planting by the Guerrilla Gardeners on May 1st.

**MITSI** is based on a design created by Liberty during the 1950s. It plays on Liberty's history with Japanese-style cherry blossom and was in the Liberty Art Fabrics autumn/winter collection of 2008 before becoming a Classic Tana Lawn.

**MITSI VALERIA** is based on a 1950s design by Gillian Farr. It references Liberty's history with Japanese-style cherry blossom designs.

**NINA TAYLOR** is a simple design of hand-painted sandalwood leaves inspired by the fragrance 'Avignon' by Comme des Garçons.

**OCEANID** is an original Liberty sketch created in the late 1980s, showing botanicals mixed with vintage objects.

**OTTILIA** is a fantastical forest design created from digitally manipulating photographs to capture Tresco Abbey Garden's diverse tropical foliage.

**PINKY** was painted by five-year-olds from St Bartholomew's School, London.

**POINTILLISM** was designed using layers of thick oil paint to create a multi-coloured texture that resembles the wildflower fields of the Tresco Abbey Garden.

**SAEED** is an eclectic mixture of hand-drawn photorealistic pansies drawn by Michael Angove and abstract violas by a student of Central Saint Martins College, London.

**SCILLY FLORA** is a tropical multi-coloured design that was inspired by the wonderful flora of the Tresco Abbey Garden.

**SMALL SUSANNA** was designed by the Liberty Design studio for the spring/summer collection of 2005. It was then re-scaled and re-coloured for the Classic Tana range in 2010.

**SPECKLE** is based on the flowers photographed at the Chelsea Flower Show, selected because of their speckled petals for the spring/summer collection of 2013.

**TRAVELLING THREADS** is a thread drawing designed by Debbie Smyth based on London Transport, created by stretching a network of threads between accurately plotted pins.

**TRESCO** is a watercolour study of a selection of flowers, ferns and succulents from the Tresco Abbey Garden.

**WILTSHIRE** is a leaf and berry pattern, which was designed for Liberty in 1933. Wiltshire has been in the Classic Tana range since 1979.

**XANTHE SUNBEAM** depicts scattered golden flora from the Tresco Abbey Garden, drawn and painted with ink in situ.

**LIBERTY**

Great Marlborough Street
London W1B 5AH
www.liberty.co.uk

Liberty fabrics are available to buy both instore and online.

**PUBLISHER'S ACKNOWLEDGEMENTS**

Thank you to Liberty for the props supplied throughout the book.

Thank you to Beg Bicycles for the loan of the bicycle on pages 57 & 60.
www.begbicycles.com